D0396654

Lillian Wald
of Henry Street

Lillian Wald of Henry Street

✦

by Beatrice Siegel

MACMILLAN PUBLISHING CO., INC.
New York

COLLIER MACMILLAN PUBLISHERS
London

In loving memory of my stepson,
Larry Siegel (1940–1969)

Frontispiece: Lillian D. Wald, about 1915
(Courtesy of Herbert L. Abrons)

Copyright © 1983 Beatrice Siegel
Macmillan Publishing Co., Inc.
866 Third Avenue, New York, N.Y. 10022
Collier Macmillan Canada, Inc.

Printed in the United States of America

Designed by Ronnie Ann Herman

10 9 8 7 6 5 4 3 2 1

Library of Congress Cataloging in Publication Data
Siegel, Beatrice.
  Lillian Wald of Henry Street.

  Includes bibliographical references and index.
  Summary: A biography of an urban pioneer who
evolved new concepts of public health, led the
movement for peace, and pressed government to
assume responsibility for the economic well-being
of its citizens.
  1. Wald, Lillian D., 1867-1940—Juvenile literature.
2. Social reformers—New York (N.Y.)—Biography—
Juvenile literature. 3. Public health nurses—
New York (N.Y.)—Biography—Juvenile literature.
4. Henry Street Settlement, New York (N.Y.)—Juvenile
literature. [1. Wald, Lillian D., 1867-1940.
2. Reformers. 3. Nurses] I. Title.
HQ1413.W34S53 1983   362.5'092'4 [B] [92]   82-20359
ISBN 0-02-782630-9

Author's Notes

My purpose originally in writing this book was to restore to the present generation a woman widely known at the turn of the century as one of this country's great urban pioneers. Lillian Wald evolved new concepts of public health, led the movement for peace, and as part of the social reform coalition, pressed government to assume responsibility for the economic well-being of its citizens. The shadings in her character became far more complex and varied as I dug into research material and interviewed people who had known her or who passed on to me, in a form of oral history, anecdotes related by parents who had known her.

In the formal nomenclature of the time, she was not called Lillian or even Lillian Wald, but Miss Wald. Or she was called The Lady. Though such forms of address are dated, I nevertheless retained them for this book for they reflect the essential formality of the period with its discreet social distancing, a period when intimacies were not easily achieved and rarely revealed.

It was personal remembrances as well as letters and papers in library archives that shaped the contents of this book. Among those I would like to thank for giving me their time and, in many instances, parting with valued photos, letters and other memorabilia, are Hermine C. Rubman, Herbert L. Abrons, Rita Sturgis Cholmeley-Jones, Louis W. Goodkind, Julius Harwood, Benjamin Schoenfein, Edith Segal, and Anna Sokolow. I would like to give special thanks to Morris Golden, the oldest survivor of the Henry Street days who at age ninety-four, now residing in Florida and blind, dictated his remembrances to an aide.

I would also like to thank the librarians and their assistants who made the Wald papers in the following collections accessible, and the directors who granted permission to quote from collections: Lillian Wald Papers, Rare Book and Manuscript Library, Columbia University; Lillian Wald Papers, Rare Books and Manuscripts Division, The New York Public Library, Astor, Lenox and Tilden Foundations; material from the Oral History Collection of Columbia University, used by permission of the Trustees of Columbia University in the City of New York. The memoirs of Isabel M. Stewart, Herbert H. Lehman, Bruno Lasker, and George W. Alger are copyright 1972; those of Adolf A. Berle are copyright 1975; The Visiting Nurse Service of New York; Nursing Archives, Special Collections, Teachers College, Columbia University; Medical Archives, New York Hospital-Cornell Medical Center; Swarthmore College Peace Collection; the Manuscript Division, Library of Congress; the New York Infirmary Archives; and the Archives, International Ladies Garment Workers' Union.

I am grateful to Professors Allen F. Davis and Gerda Lerner who read the manuscript and, in critical comments, gave me the benefit of their scholarship. Professor Blanche Wiesen Cook, in several wide-ranging discussions, helped me gain better understanding of the period.

I would also like to thank Jane Sherman Lehac who read the work-in-progress, suggested revisions, and urged me on. My husband, Sam Siegel, was invaluable as an assistant in countless ways, and my daughter, Andra Patterson, put her special research skills into this work.

New York City
June, 1982

Contents

1

The Old World
and the New

H E R family moved so often, it hardly mattered to Lillian Wald where she was born and grew up. People were important, not places. Still, in the mid-nineteenth century the Ohio valley where she spent her childhood was different in character from the densely populated cities of the eastern seaboard. Though the frontier had pushed farther into the West, the valley continued to draw the adventurous, those with restless energy and drive.

For the thousands of people arriving from Germany and Poland in 1849, among them Lillian's family, the eastern cities no longer presented opportunities for economic and social mobility. In search of better lives, ambitious immigrants as well as the native born worked their way to the Midwest. They traveled by railroads newly spanning the country, and in wagons over the Appalachian Mountains, or by boat and barge along Lake Erie in the north. Some traveled down the Ohio, a mighty river that originated in Pennsylvania, flowed south and west to form the southern rim of the state that bore its name, and joined the Mississippi.

There was so much land that no one had to fight for space. Over the years the newcomers carved farms out of the rich soil and built roads, schools, and churches. Along river routes they set up industries and turned commercial centers into cities.

People of different religious beliefs felt an exhilarating sense of freedom in the Ohio valley. Initiative and ambition counted, who you were becoming, *not* who you were. Jewish immigrants like Lillian's family, sheltered within the growing Midwestern cities, felt the unique experience of social acceptance. They decided, optimistically, that they had seen the future and that religious discrimination was coming to an end. In 1854, Cincinnati became the center of Reform Judaism in the new world, when worshipers there in the oldest congregation in Ohio began to express advanced theological ideas. They agreed that the times were favorable to give up customs that differentiated them from their Christian neighbors and to merge, or assimilate with them.

Lillian, born in Cincinnati on March 10, 1867, lived her childhood in this liberating climate. She was the equal of children in the neighborhood and if her parents so wished could go to public school with them. Both outside the home and within the circle of her large family she had a profound sense of being secure and loved. In the household were her parents, her oldest brother, Alfred, her sister, Julia, and after Lillian came Gustavus, the baby brother whom they all called Gus.

Through the windows of her home she could look out at the splendor of open space, uncluttered land that extended as far as she could see. A few steps outside her door and she was in the family garden and flower beds enjoying the glow of color that came with fresh blossoms. From her mother Lillian inherited a love for flowers and she would surround herself with them wherever she lived.

Lillian's father and mother had been children themselves when they were brought to the United States. Her mother, Minnie Schwarz, came from Germany, her father, Marcus D. Wald, from Poland. Both descended from a long line of well-to-do men and women over whom a king or prince might, at a whim, relax laws regulating where Jews could live and work. Anti-Semitic restrictions were, however, generally fixed as if graven in stone. Jews, forced to direct talent and brains into only a few occupations, soon excelled in their endeavors. Lillian's forebears succeeded as merchants, rabbis, scholars, and professionals. There is some evidence that Lillian's father was descended from a Rabbi Wahl who was also the ancestor of the German composer Felix Mendelssohn. But Mendelssohn could perform his works in the courts of Europe only because his father had converted to Christianity and he was known as a "Christian Jew."

When the revolutionary uprisings in central Europe in 1848-49 failed, the Schwarz and Wald families joined thousands of others fleeing from their homelands. They knew that in the wake of such upheaval would come new persecutions against Jews, political repression, and economic turmoil. The brutal ocean crossing did not dim their courage and they pushed on past the coastal cities to the Midwest.

Minnie was only sixteen when she married Max, as Marcus was called. They may have had similar ancestries but it seemed to Lillian that it was a marriage of opposites. Her mother was attractive, lively, colorful, always walking into the house with an armful of roses she had cut in the garden, or chrysanthemums and lilies she had bought in a nearby greenhouse. Her father, on the other hand, was quiet, retiring, somewhat in the manner of his Polish ancestors who had studied their holy books.

While her mother sometimes seemed faraway and remote, more often she was warm and trusting, drawing people to her. She looked enchanting, delicate of feature, slim, graceful. Lillian, even as a child, felt protective toward her mother, especially when she found her reclining on a sofa with one of her frequent headaches. At such times, her mother would ask Lillian to read the newspapers to her and the child would catch a view of the politics, corruption, and violence taking place in the expanding cities. Lillian could not remember when she did not love to read, dramatically identifying with the characters in the Charles Dickens or George Eliot novels she fastened onto at one period. When a physician advised rest for her inflamed eyes, she hid under the piano with a favorite book and read undiscovered for hours.

For practical advice, Lillian would turn to her father, and she would regret in later years that she did not get to know him better. It would have been difficult, not only because he was so retiring, but also because he often traveled for business, selling optical supplies.

On occasion her father took the family with him. Lillian cherished a few memories of such trips, of riding down the Mississippi River in a steamboat, and of sitting in a hotel room enjoying the sumptuous breakfast of fresh eggs, milk, and cheese her father had fetched from a nearby farm, rather than have his children eat the hotel food he considered inedible.

Her mother, off in her own world as she might on occasion appear to be, nevertheless managed the large household with the aid of a servant. She brought to it her warmth and good taste, and the added sparkle of her convivial family. Lillian would see her father fade into a large living room chair after dinner and look on over his metal-rimmed spectacles while her mother and Schwarz relatives shared excited talk on many subjects.

Lillian's Grandfather Schwarz and Uncle Samuel visited so often that she considered them part of her family. They enchanted her with Old World tales. Grandfather Schwarz, whose first name—Gutman—became Goodman in Ohio, recalled stories of German legend and history and told the children about the adventures of the *Arabian Nights*. He also taught them about their Jewish origin through stories from the Bible. Uncle Samuel, her mother's brother, recited reams of lines from Shakespeare, gave theatrical recitations about the Roman Emperor Marcus Aurelius, and read the Psalms of David.

She recalled her uncle as a curious figure, a pathetic as well as a dashing and brilliant man. She would see her mother drop whatever she was doing to give him her full attention as soon as he entered the house. Her father, too, would leap from his chair and offer it to Uncle Samuel. He was a physician who early in his career had almost died from an overdose of a drug he had prescribed for himself. His lack of judgment, or lack of knowledge, so unnerved him that he gave up the practice of medicine rather than risk endangering anyone's life. Lillian would remember him, not for his invalidism (in which condition he lived to be ninety-two), but for his stories and the books he brought her.

She called her Grandfather Schwarz—Favey. He was a beloved figure, almost a surrogate father, a proud man with a steady gaze, crisp gray hair, sideburns and mustache. Favey, who had taken his wife and five children on the long trek from rural Germany to Ohio, was a heroic figure to his grandchildren. Always an energetic entrepreneur, he put his commercial wizardry to work and became a successful merchant in Ohio, dealing in tar and other commodities. And he liked nothing better than to indulge his grandchildren. He gave them gifts of ponies, one of which was always yellow with a black mane and tail whom the children named Kitty. He brought them caged birds and a few days later released them and let them fly away. When he funded a group of touring German actors to perform in plays by German dramatist Friedrich Schiller, Lillian and the other children took their friends to performances to help fill up the house. Though none of them understood a word of German, treats to ice cream after the shows made the evenings worthwhile. And the outdoor playhouse Favey built for the children was large enough for Lillian to play in; she would stand at the small stove to prepare bottles of milk for her dolls, and gaze outside the playhouse window onto a path bordered with flowers.

Favey had carefully reproduced in the playhouse the architecture, landscaping, and furniture of a typical house in rural Germany. He missed his homeland and he had only happy memories of his life there.

When Lillian grew older, she understood more fully a story her grandfather told about his Uncle Karl, a physician at the court of a prince. Uncle Karl fell in love with a lady-in-waiting. In order to marry her, he gave up his Jewish faith and became a Christian. It was all right to change one's religion for love, Favey had said, for above all, Lillian's grandfather had an ability to accommodate to reality. That ability made it possible for his family to prosper despite anti-Semitic restrictions, and Favey related only cheerful experiences of his life in a small German town. He was a man of buoyant spirit, confident and optimistic. Lillian absorbed these qualities and made them her own for a lifetime.

Even as a child, she was winning, energetic, and bright. The dramatic flair with which she regaled her friends with Favey's stories when they gathered on the front porch convinced her mother that Lillian would become a writer.

Her favorite friend in those growing-up years was her brother Alfred, a kindred spirit in boldness and imagination. He put together a newspaper, and directed theatrical productions for the children in which he naturally played the lead. And when Lillian's favorite doll became hopelessly sick and died, Alfred led the funeral oration. Lillian had dressed her doll in white, and with Alfred's help, intoned the proper ritual and buried it in a garden plot. (When it rained a few days later, her mother dug it up and restored it to health.) The child could stand up to her older brother as she did one rainy day on their walk to school. She snatched the umbrella from him, calling him selfish for not shielding her from the downpour. When the rain soaked through his clothes, she regretted her action and deliberately kept the umbrella closed, becoming as drenched as he.

Alfred excelled in so many ways that his family had high hopes for him. It consoled Lillian to think she would follow him to the ends of the earth. Her older sister, Julia, also attractive and lively, was more accepting of the conventions of that time. Baby brother Gus trailed along after the others.

Attached to each child's name at birth was the initial "D," as if it were a talisman to bring good luck. It was part of their father's name and stood for nothing but itself, a letter.

Thus it was Lillian D. Wald who grew to womanhood first in Cincinnati, then in Dayton, Ohio, and finally in Rochester, New York, where the family moved in 1878. Eleven-year-old Lillian was excited at the prospect of moving to a larger city where she had many cousins, aunts, and uncles. Though she was only slightly acquainted with them, there had always been a generous exchange of gifts on birthdays and special occasions.

While her parents searched for a suitable home, she lodged with relatives. Cousins took her for walks on treelined streets and along the banks of the Genesee river that wound through the town. In the springtime Rochester burst into bloom and she understood why it was called the "flower city." German and Irish immigrants had built 2,000 acres of greenhouses and nurseries, making Rochester the seed basket for the Midwest farmlands. As a gift to the city, nursery owners beautified Rochester by contributing land for a park and planting its slopes with hundreds of varieties of lilac. Rochester was a spectacle of fragrant, colorful blossoms when magnolia and lilac burst into flower in parks, lawns, and small backyards.

The move to Rochester had been, above all, for practical purposes. The city had become the center for optical supplies, making it easier for Lillian's father to carry on his business. Her mother was lured by family—two brothers and a sister lived in Rochester, all of them in the clothing industry. The Schwarz Brothers, Henry and Morris, had become one of Rochester's earliest and most successful firms. Another leading manufacturer, Michael, Levi and Company, was headed by Lillian's uncle by marriage to her maternal aunt. They were people of status and wealth, lauded for bringing renewed economic vitality to a city that had been blighted by years of economic depression.

The Walds finally moved into their own home on fashionable East Avenue and took up the routine of comfortable middle-class lives. They stayed there only a couple of years and then relocated to South Union Street where they spent a few years in a house right next door to Lillian's Uncle Henry.

The family continued to support Reform Judaism and welcomed Christian ministers to the Jewish temple. In this liberal religious atmosphere Lillian never developed a strong sense of Jewish identity. She was assimilated further into the social life of the city when she was sent to Miss Cruttenden's, a prestigious, nonsectarian school that accepted referrals from Christian sources as well as from Dr. Max Landsberg, head of the Reform Jewish temple.

Lillian was sometimes a day student and at other times she boarded at Miss Cruttenden's. Called an "English and French Boarding and Day School for Young Ladies and Little Girls," Miss

Cruttenden ran one of the better schools in Rochester and turned out disciplined, educated young women. Without too much effort, Lillian excelled in languages, music and the arts, and showed considerable interest in math and science as well. She was not a loner, buried in her books, but lively, popular, surrounded by friends. Tall (five foot six) and regal looking, she wore her dark hair piled on top of her head. ". . . how stunning you were when going out," recalled a younger student. "I especially remember a blue satin, with your evening coat and party bag. We thought you the most beautiful girl we had ever seen." The next day, when Lillian reported on her dancing partners to the younger generation as she had promised, her popularity was assured.

Miss Cruttenden was also forward looking. She announced in her brochure the establishment of a college preparatory department to "fit" pupils for Vassar, Wellesley, Bryn Mawr, and Smith. In the 1880s, few parents shared the view that their daughters should go on to college. They regarded that as a privilege for men who had access to the outer world. In their conventional circles, the school's purpose was to enhance their daughters' opportunities to be future wives and mothers.

Lillian, too, was being groomed for her role in society, a future that could only have looked bleak to her. The outside world attracted her and not marriage. She could listen to her brother Alfred plan a life of adventure and know she would live such a life only in her imagination, or through his experiences. She shared the family's expectation that, like Uncle Samuel, Alfred would study medicine. Lillian saw herself as his trusted aide, working at his side, caring for the sick. But Alfred chose a life of his own and instead of going to college, he joined his uncles in the clothing industry. Lillian, frustrated at this turn of events, had to fall back on her own resources. Her immediate plan was to attend college herself, and at sixteen, she applied to Vassar in Poughkeepsie, New York. She was rejected, as she would recall in later years, because she was too young. That single rejection put an end to further thoughts of a college education. Discouraged, she continued at Miss Cruttenden's for another two years, dutifully pursuing her studies, helping out at home, and going on a dismal round of teas and dances. And then, she had to put aside her own needs for a terrible blow struck the family.

Uncle Samuel Schwarz had opened a clothing store in California after his failed professional career. When he decided to take a three-month cure abroad at a spa in Baden-Baden, he asked Alfred to take charge of his business. Alfred agreed and remained in California while Uncle Samuel's three months in Europe stretched into a year and a half. On May 30, 1885, the Wald family received a telegram that Alfred had drowned. He was twenty-five years old.

The agony that followed receipt of the telegram forced Lillian's mother to bed for months. When again she resumed her place in the household, it was with eyes shadowed forever with grief. Lillian tried to stay close to home but she desperately needed relief from her own feelings of loss and bewilderment and decided to take a job. For a few months she found temporary escape in doing clerical work in an uncle's firm. Then she began a two-year stint as a correspondent for the Bradstreet Company, investigating the financial credentials of business firms. The fact that she could carry on this kind of work at home made it easier for her conventional family to accept a working daughter. But both jobs were boring and in no way satisfied her need to be actively challenged.

In May 1888, she participated in the elaborate preparations for her sister Julia's marriage to Charles P. Barry, son of a wealthy Irish family, the founders of Rochester's largest nursery and seed company. After a few years the Barrys moved into a custom-built, Georgian-style home on East Avenue. Wherever Lillian turned she was surrounded by the accouterments of elegant taste. Favey, too, had moved to Rochester and had become a collector of antique silver and furniture, showering the family with gifts. Her mother had a single hope: that young, beautiful Lillian would follow Julia's example into a gracious marriage.

The pressures to conform were building up all around her. How simple it would have been if marriage were her goal as it had been her sister's and cousins' and friends'! It was not as if she rejected marriage because she felt some lofty calling to which she wanted to devote her life. That was not it. Many men were attracted to her, yet she was not attracted to them. She did not understand her own feelings except that she had the need to do something—to free herself from feeling isolated, closed in, as if she were locked into a cocoon from which she could not emerge.

In the secret of her days there was often the panic of uncertainty, of emptiness, of being adrift. She had not gone to college as a new generation of middle-class women had; she had no profession, no career, no training. And in rejecting the traditional feminine role defined by the circles in which she moved, she was without direction. She must have wondered why she was different. Perhaps she could have said, as the poet Walt Whitman did when he faced his own inner nature,

> ... I have not once had the least idea who or what I am,
> But that before all my insolent poems, the real Me still stands untouched, untold, altogether unreached.

2

A New Woman

N O T only did she feel closed in by her own sense of being different, but her family, despite its many virtues, was detached and aloof from the intellectual ferment around them. It seemed to her she went on the same dreary round to family gatherings where the talk was always about business. Yet she read in the newspapers about dramatic changes, about industrialization and private enterprise and men who were taking over land and resources, changing the face of the country, the economy, and politics. She was as amused as the public at large by stories of wasteful, extravagant entertainments that became scandalous when the newly rich filled palatial homes with the contents of European castles. Mark Twain called the era the Gilded Age to describe the rot beneath the glitter, for it was common knowledge that fraud and corruption pervaded every level of government and commerce.

Her restlessness made her seek the world beyond the narrow circle of her middle-class family and friends. On the periphery of her mind she was aware that millions of immigrants were flooding the country in the 1880s. They came to build the railroads, tunnels, bridges; they worked in the mines; they used the new, fast, steam-powered machines in textile mills and clothing factories. And because government favored the industrialists, giving them unbridled liberties to accumulate profits, workers had to fight to survive. The poverty of millions was brushed aside by the philosophic concept of the day, laissez faire, which sanctioned freedom for industrialists from government interference.

Lillian might have been living in a castle surrounded by a moat, so little did she understand the explosive conditions that existed in Rochester and that affected her extended family. Rochester was becoming industrialized, especially in the clothing industry where her uncles, among others, had introduced new machinery and employed cheap labor supplied by the thousand or so immigrants who had settled there. Among the newcomers were Jews fleeing the ghettos of Russia and Poland. Though they shared the same religion as Lillian's German-Jewish family, they were alien in every other way. Coming from impoverished towns, many of these slight men and women were unkempt and illiterate and spoke a strange language, Yiddish. Rochester's native-born and earlier settlers made them the butt of ridicule and scorn. But when the ridicule blew up into undisguised anti-Semitism, the German-Jewish community stepped in and publicly claimed support for the people of their faith. In private, however, the Jewish elite expressed resentment at being identified with these peculiar Jewish immigrants who tarnished their hard-won image and threatened their foothold in mainstream America.

Lillian did her share of good works for the relief of the poor. She danced evenings away at fancy balls on behalf of the Hebrew Benevolent Association and other organizations where the wealthy gathered. And she saw her impulsively generous mother help every needy person who begged on the street or rang the doorbell.

But she did not come directly into contact with the poor. Nor did the drama of poverty unfolding on the other side of town arouse her sympathy. The poor were someplace out there, strange, inscrutable people who lived in slums and worked in factories.

One woman who lived in a slum and worked in a factory had a great deal to say about her life in Rochester, so different from Lillian Wald's. Lillian was eighteen years old when sixteen-year-old Emma Goldman arrived from Russia to join her sister, an earlier immigrant. Miss Goldman called Rochester "flower city for the rich." The American Beauty roses in a vase on her boss's desk cost more than her weekly wage. She had found a job at Garson's, a "model" clothing factory, where she sewed buttons on heavy overcoats for ten and a half hours a day, six days a week. Her weekly wage of $2.50 did not cover her food and board. But more insufferable was the "iron discipline," as she called it, of plant foremen who made sure she and the other workers did not move from their machines. They even had to ask permission to go to the toilet.

Her work sapped her energy and made thousands of young women in the work force old at an early age, Miss Goldman said. These conditions enraged her and she met with other workers in dingy basement flats to talk about trade union organization and strikes, and about socialism and anarchism. Miss Goldman attended union meetings that demanded an eight-hour work day, and she was taking her first steps toward becoming a leading anarchist. She believed that the state and its apparatus were coercive and should be abolished and that people, in free agreement among themselves, would be able to resolve the social and economic problems of society. Miss Goldman eventually left Rochester, but other immigrants stayed on to become the backbone of Rochester's clothing industry. In the 1880s, when Lillian was in her teens, seamstresses led strikes against "speedups and low wages" through a new organization, the Protective Union and Mutual Aid Society. The strike spread to all the factories, including those owned by Lillian's uncles.

Lillian had no way of experiencing this labor uprising or the demands for change led by a crusader who lived nearby. Miss Susan B. Anthony was heading campaigns for woman suffrage and equal rights from the modest family homestead she shared with her sister right off the center of town. (The same house had been a station on the underground railroad during the fight against slavery.) Years before Lillian Wald moved to Rochester, Miss Anthony had led a group of women to the polls in that city to test their right to vote. Her arrest and trial for voting illegally created such public uproar that she was never put in jail though she refused to pay the $100 fine.

But more than Miss Anthony's crusades and Miss Goldman's anarchism were shaking up the old social order. The magazines and newspapers Lillian read told her about new voices, women's voices, fighting to be heard in the Gilded Age. Women were demanding the vote, jobs, college educations, the right to become professionals, to put their skills to productive, creative uses. They led union struggles, formed clubs, and spoke out on many issues. In the Women's Christian Temperance Union, thousands of women banded together to exert political and social power in their fight to end drunkenness and family abuse; and they began to tackle the brutal conditions among the poor, exposing the evils of industrial society. A young Jane Addams, a pioneer in the settlement house movement, summed it up neatly in 1880 when she said woman was passing "from the arts of pleasing, to the development of intellectual forces and her capabilities for direct labor."

Lillian had had mild exposure to liberal thought. Grandfather Favey had taken her to lectures to hear the "Great Agnostic," Robert Ingersoll, and the celebrated minister Henry Ward Beecher, a supporter of woman suffrage. And she had made a movement toward independence when she held a job. Struggling with her own needs, she drew courage from the new ideas in ferment around her. At least she was not alone in rejecting an idle, passive life. She was twenty-two when she found a way out of her paralyzing feelings of uncertainty. It came about after the family moved again, in 1888, this time to Fostoria, Ohio, where her brother Gus had settled. She was saved from the monotony of the backwater town by spending most of her time in Rochester with her sister and brother-in-law, the Barrys.

During her visit, Julia was ill in her first pregnancy and was under a doctor's care. He asked that a nurse be put on the case. Lillian, eager to be helpful, offered to fetch her.

In the return walk to the Barry home, Lillian questioned the young woman, not much older than she, about her training at the Bellevue Hospital School of Nursing in New York City. And while this nurse and others were in the Barry home, Lillian continued to ask questions. She observed them in their crisp uniforms carrying out a round of duties, caring for the patient, making beds, cleaning. She learned that nursing required special training, that it was disciplined, hard work. She also observed that her family disdained nursing and regarded it as only a level above domestic work.

But in Lillian's mind a daring idea had formed. She saw in nursing a door opening onto a possible career. Compassion for the sick was hardly the compelling force; instead, she felt nursing might meet other needs—to find out who she was, to feel useful, to be independent, to move away from the smothering narrowness of her life. And there *was* something noble about nursing; was it not nurturing and healing, women's arts?

Her decision gave her a feeling of liberation. She saw an end to the daily acts of compliance that bound her life to conventions she did not respect. And though she cared deeply for her family, especially her mother, she would not accede to their wish that she study nursing in Rochester. It was as important to remove herself from the family as it was to train for a career.

She explained her reasons for wishing to attend school in New York to Mr. George P. Ludlum, superintendent of New York Hospital, in her application to its School of Nursing. Though it is written from Fostoria, Ohio, in May, 1889, she refers to life in Rochester.

"I have many social ties in Rochester, which might interfere with earnest, uninterrupted work there," she wrote. About her qualifications, she noted that she has "had the advantages of what might be called a good education, knowing Latin, and able to speak both French and German. . . . My life hitherto has been . . . a type of modern American young womanhood, days devoted to society, study and housekeeping duties such as practical mothers consider essential to a daughter's education.

"This does not satisfy me now," she continued. "I feel the need of serious, definite work. A need perhaps more apparent since the desire to become a professional nurse has had birth. I choose this profession because I feel a natural aptitude for it and because it has for years appeared to me womanly, congenial work, work that I love and which I think I could do well."

Mr. Ludlum asked Lillian to come in for an interview. In the summer of 1889, while she was living with the Barrys at their sea-shore home, her brother-in-law Charles accompanied her to New York City. The School of Nursing of New York Hospital was then located at West Fifteenth Street off Fifth Avenue.

She was interviewed by Miss Irene H. Sutliffe, an 1880 graduate in charge of nursing education. Miss Sutliffe guided Lillian on a tour of the hospital, through large sunny rooms with scrubbed tile floors and shining brass fixtures hanging from high ceilings. But when she saw the sick children, each in a separate crib in a large ward, she was overcome with pity and winced at the sight of a young boy in braces. Miss Sutliffe caught Lillian's reaction and gave her the first important lesson in nursing. "That boy is not suffering," she said. "He is a hero in the ward, and if you come you and he will have great fun together."

There was no pity in Miss Sutliffe's voice, only an acceptance of a different situation—a child in braces but an individual nonetheless.

Lillian was elated at the interview and if her parents thought a visit to a hospital, her first, would cool her ardor, it had the opposite effect. More determined than ever to become a nurse, she decided she would apply to schools in Rochester in the event she was turned down by the New York School of Nursing. It was with relief that she received a notice of acceptance. She would be admitted for the fall term of August, 1889, and only after a month's probation could she become a full student.

Her first days as a student nurse put her on trial. She found herself living in a tiny, dark, windowless room, as if she was doing penance in a nunnery. Thorne Mansion, in which she was housed, was once a fashionable private home that had been converted to nurses' quarters. The building, located on the south side of West Sixteenth Street off Fifth Avenue, was structurally connected to New York Hospital, situated directly in back of it on West Fifteenth Street.

Making her room even eerier were the cooing sounds of caged doves that drifted down during the night from the solarium one floor above. During the day the solarium was really a cheerful room, filled with plants, and a tank of goldfish in addition to caged doves and owls. Convalescent patients used the room for a daytime smoke. In the evenings when she had leisure, Lillian met other students there for relaxation.

She started to work immediately and slowly adapted to basic training which consisted of a repetition of menial tasks. She was educated more in the use of her hands than her mind. The hospital had 1,000 in-patients and hundreds of out-patients who used the basement clinic. She put in an exhausting twelve-hour day learning to care for them, in an existence completely stripped of accustomed comforts. As a probationer, she was taught how to make bandages and dressings, and how to sterilize instruments. She became adept at "cupping" and applying mustard plasters, procedures common in those days in the care of the sick. She did grimy scrub work, washed dishes, polished brass, made beds, handled emergencies, and did simple cooking. A skimpy theoretical training was provided in anatomy, physiology, chemistry, and other medical subjects through lectures given irregularly by the medical staff. When she had time, she learned to dissect ox eyes, cats, and dogs in the laboratory.

All this output of energy was done on poor, inadequate meals and crowded living quarters! "Strenuous years," she would write in her book, *House on Henry Street*, "for an undisciplined, untrained girl, but a wonderful human experience."

After she passed the month's probation, Lillian was moved into better quarters and was also rewarded with the privilege of wearing a blue plaid uniform that covered her from neck to ankle. The fine fabric, made in Scotland exclusively for the school, was a special touch added by Miss Sutliffe, director of nursing.

Over her uniform, Lillian wore a long white apron, a belt from which hung keys, a thermometer case, scissors, and other instruments she needed on her rounds. Completing her outfit was the traditional white starched cap she pinned tightly to her thick hair.

The uniform, the sturdy shoes that encased her feet, were the outer garments, symbols of a demanding profession that was slowly changing the inner person. She had personal problems to overcome; she was impulsive and squeamish at the sight of pain. She avoided going up to surgery. Miss Sutliffe, who helped her with these difficulties, was a woman of rare qualities. Petite without being fragile, and gracious in manner, she tempered discipline with warmth and insight.

"It will give Mrs. Finegan courage to have you at her side," Miss Sutliffe explained to Nurse Wald when a favorite patient was due for an operation. Nurse Wald took Mrs. Finegan up to surgery and stayed on to help in the surgical procedures. Again she learned that pity, especially self-pity, had no place in nursing.

And it had been a long, slow process learning to curb her impulses, generous and well-meaning though they seemed to her. Lillian always remembered an incident that occurred during her first few days at nursing school. She had gone down to the basement on an errand and heard wild shouting coming from behind a closed door. She rushed over, opened the door, and was shocked to find an elderly man in a padded cell raving that he was hungry and deliberately being starved. Outraged at such cruelty, and having no one to turn to on that particular Sunday afternoon, she appealed to the elevator man. He, already fond of Nurse Wald, handed her the keys to the diet kitchen where she raided the icebox of prepared food and fed the starving man. The next day, feeling every bit a heroine, she reported the experience to Miss Sutliffe.

Miss Sutliffe listened calmly and then explained that the man, a habitual drunkard, had been placed in isolation to "dry out," that the food she removed had been specially prepared for sick patients who consequently had nothing to eat, and that Nurse Wald would have to learn that certain hospital procedures are essential. And then, to cheer up the crestfallen young heroine, Miss Sutliffe told her in confidence that she was glad Miss Wald had fed the old scoundrel rather than let him go hungry.

Miss Sutliffe had from the first perceived her student's energy and warmth. And she kept in mind Miss Cruttenden's letter of recommendation that Lillian Wald "has fine qualities . . . intelligence, amiability, high principles, and excitement."

That "amiability" and "excitement" made her a nursing treasure, popular with patients who looked for her cheerfulness and her interest in their problems. Colleagues would remember her "creative drive," an extraordinary ability to bring into focus what had to be done and then getting it accomplished.

And in the year and a half program, Nurse Wald had every reason to confirm that she had chosen a noble calling. She was in the company of bright women, twenty-five to thirty-five years of age (to qualify, Lillian had told a little lie to which she later confessed, claiming she was twenty-five instead of twenty-two), who chose nursing as one of the few careers available to them in the 1880s. Whatever personal reasons brought them to the school—the need to earn a living, a preference for a career rather than marriage, a different form of comradeship, or a simple need to feel useful—she found her colleagues capable and courageous, defying the conventional thinking of the times. And she was one of them, a new woman, connecting, growing in self-confidence as she developed a skill. In the "sisterhood," as nursing was called, she made lifelong friends. The gentle Mary Maud Brewster was one of them. Five foot ten, slender as a wisp, with a small face, blue eyes and blond hair, Miss Brewster was almost too fragile for her chosen profession. She had been raised in Montrose, New Jersey, where her father, Andrew Jackson Brewster, was a blacksmith and a church elder. The family was descended from the Pilgrim leader Reverend William Brewster.

Anne Warburton Goodrich was also a member of the sisterhood and Lillian Wald's friend. Miss Goodrich was as tall as Miss Wald, five foot six, and like her, the product of a private school education, but she had completed her studies abroad and her wealthy family accepted her need to be independent. She combined rare administrative ability with a strong will and a sense of humor, and even as a student she showed promise of leadership.

Miss Wald and her colleagues learned whatever techniques were available at the time and could take care of a wide range of medical illnesses, often doing the same work as young doctors. In health circles they were regarded as saviors who would heal the sick and improve society by wiping out the causes of disease.

Florence Nightingale had set the tone for nursing, declaring it an art that required exclusive devotion. Less than forty years before, Miss Nightingale had removed nursing from the sentimental attitudes clinging to it, cut its church affiliations, and made it secular. She attracted women to this new profession by declaring it a life of "complete satisfaction and worth-whileness for those who would work hard." She modernized nursing and nudged men out of controlling administrative positions, appointing women who she insisted must be trained, competent nurses. Essential to good health, according to Miss Nightingale, were cleanliness, pure air and water, proper lighting, and healthy food.

Nurse Wald was armed with a practical skill and Florence Nightingale's concepts when she was graduated in March, 1891. At Miss Sutliffe's request, she stayed on to train incoming students. After only two months in her new position, she received a call notifying her of her father's sudden death.

Throughout her year and a half as a student nurse, she had visited home, always assuring her family that she was pleased with her work. Though her mother still had more traditional goals for her, her father, steadfast in his devotion, had accepted her search for independence. In his quiet way he was proud of her accomplishments.

This May, 1891, on her lonely voyage back to Rochester where her parents had again settled, she quietly mourned her father's death. And concern for her mother, for her pain and loneliness, filled her with anxiety. She considered the possibility of offering to return home to live, to share the family household. But in New York she had gained her freedom, not only through a profession, but through meeting resourceful and independent women mapping out new directions. She was beginning to feel the force of her own energy now that it was channeled and focused. And she could talk of loving and being loved, when years of living in Rochester had produced no warm relationships.

She need not have suffered such conflict, for her sister and brother-in-law invited Mrs. Wald to live with them. Lillian spent months with her mother and helped her close her home and pack away cartons of childhood pictures, letters, the bits and pieces of family treasures, to be stored at Julia's. When she saw her mother comfortably settled, she returned to New York in August, 1891, to undertake her first job as a professional nurse.

3

A Weeping Child

THOUGH she had her choice of many such openings, it had never been her intention to become a private duty nurse concerned with the care of a single patient. The idea of working within a larger community, especially one charged with the care of children, appealed to her. And she looked forward, upon her return to New York, to her position as a staff nurse at the New York Juvenile Asylum on West 176 Street.

Her excitement was stillborn when, in a painful awakening, she learned the nature of institutional life. She found orphaned and unwanted children thrown together with petty criminals remanded to the Asylum for reform. One thousand such youngsters ranging in age between five and eighteen were housed in a complex of stone buildings as cold and forbidding within as was the high fence outdoors that enclosed the structures onto four acres of land.

The injustice and consistent abuse she witnessed outraged her. She spoke up on one occasion and demanded a fair trial for a child found guilty of a theft without a hearing. On another she accompanied a young boy with a toothache to the Asylum dentist who, without a preliminary examination, prepared to pull the tooth. Only when she threatened to take the youngster to her own dentist, did he examine the child's mouth and find that the tooth could be saved after all.

The children cleaned, cooked, farmed, or did factory work on a work-training program. They turned out suits, shoes, and dresses for the Asylum population. Bleary-eyed, they were hardly able to learn the basics of reading and writing taught in the classroom. As a witness to their plight, Miss Wald realized that children could be permanently damaged by poverty and institutional life.

It seemed hopeless to stay on, for she was realist enough to know that she might win a skirmish or two, but would not be able to change the entrenched abuse.

She left her job after a year and went downtown to entroll at the Woman's Medical College for the fall term of 1892. Even if she did not become a physician, it seemed a good idea to broaden her medical knowledge. At least the College, located in lower Manhattan at Livingston Place and Stuyvesant Square, brought her closer to her friends at the New York School of Nursing. And there was a refreshing ambience at the College, which was part of the New York Infirmary for Women and Children two doors away.

Again, as in the School of Nursing, she was moving in a woman's world. She knew that Elizabeth Blackwell had founded both the Infirmary and the College after her own experience of being turned down by twenty-eight colleges for the study of medicine because she was a woman. A small medical college in upstate New York finally admitted her and she rewarded them by graduating at the head of the class. She took two years additional study in Europe where she became a friend of Florence Nightingale and accepted her concepts that sanitation and good environment were essential to health.

Upon her return to New York from Europe, Miss Blackwell found that circumstances had not changed. She was the first woman doctor in the United States and instead of being honored, she was rebuffed and vilified. Landlords refused her rooms for a private practice; the medical profession denied her the use of hospital wards though such affiliation was essential for experience; she was labeled a fraud; and called "that weird little doctress."

Little she was, but also slender and pleasant looking and every inch a fighter. The same determination that gained her admission to medical school carried her forward. For years she struggled to support herself by giving lectures and classes. After running a small dispensary on the Lower East Side, she was able to found the medical college and hospital where women could study, practice their profession, or come to be examined by doctors of their own sex.

For months Miss Wald involved herself in the routine of classwork, studying physics, chemistry, anatomy, physiology, and doing practical work in the dissecting laboratories. At no time in her life had she studied so intensely, and though she did well, academic work demanded solitude and that did not appeal to her. She wanted the warmth of working with people. But studying at the medical college provided more than academics; she was among dozens of women undertaking careers long denied them. Implemented were the words of the main speaker at a school graduation who had said, women should not be debarred from "any function which their brain and strength enabled them to perform."

At times such as these, when she was uncertain about her goals, she missed her family. She was still mourning Favey's death a few months before. She had returned home to join her mother and Julia in the ritual period of grief, recalling with them the pleasures and certainties of an earlier age.

Back in New York, taking classes, marking time, meeting impressive women, she was being tempered in unexpected ways. Each day when she left her comfortable student quarters to go to class, she saw lines of poor sick people patiently waiting to get into the infirmary. She saw them in the ten clinic rooms in the basement of the Medical College, just as she had seen them crowd the wards of New York Hospital when she was a student nurse.

In Rochester, the poor had been invisible, a strange, shabby group whom she had secretly scorned. Though her family gave to the needy, it was always through impersonalized charitable organizations.

The abstract mass was now turning into visibly distressed people —men, women, and children in queer old clothes, the women with sick babies in their arms and scrawny toddlers clutching their skirts. She saw their flushed, feverish faces, running noses, and heard their dry, racking coughs. Most of them were immigrants, desperately lost and bewildered in an alien country. They came to the clinics from the most densely populated twenty-block strip of land in the United States—perhaps in the world—the Lower East Side.

Alive to a new reality, she volunteered to teach a class in home care and hygiene offered to immigrant women. The sponsor of the class was Mrs. Solomon (Betty) Loeb, a well-known philanthropist.

One morning each week Miss Wald traveled down to the Louis Technical School at 267 Henry Street, beginning an odyssey that would change the course of her life. Exploding around her were chaotic scenes of poverty, vitality, degradation, and spirit so unique that a later resident would call the Lower East Side an "autonomous republic."

As she let her mind absorb these impressions, she perceived the immigrants in truer context. Millions were arriving in a steady stream from impoverished towns of Europe and making that corner of New York their first stop. They were packed into dank, airless tenement rooms like ramshackle pieces of furniture in a warehouse. These firetraps they called homes had broken-down wooden stairs, evil-smelling outdoor toilets, rarely a bathtub, and often no running water. The streets she explored were crammed with shops, pushcarts, and peddlers hawking bargains in soap and needles. The hectic commerce was interlaced with piles of rotting garbage, horse-drawn wagons, and fire escapes strewn with household possessions. Though the Jewish language rang out in the crowded streets, she heard a medley of other tongues that announced the mixed nationalities in the community—Italian, Russian, Hungarian, Rumanian, Irish, Polish. Neither flower nor tree sparked the landscape with color—only people crowded into every bit of space.

In a small room in the school on Henry Street, Miss Wald faced a group of women who barely understood English. Their young, tired faces, their eagerness to learn the simplest lessons on sanitation and good health, brought out her tenderest feelings. In her few years in New York, her middle-class prejudices had gradually peeled away, like dead skin, and she could now relate to these people as individuals. They had their own pride and dignity and needed from Miss Wald the benefits of her training, not her pity.

In the midst of demonstrating one morning how to make beds with sheets she had brought with her, a weeping child timidly entered the room to explain to Miss Wald why her mother could not come to class.

"My mother is sick," said the child.

Miss Wald looked down into the tear-streaked, frightened face, snatched up the sheets and followed the child out of the classroom into the rain. She walked with the child over the broken-down roadways of Hester and Division streets, "between tall reeking houses . . . past evil smelling, uncovered garbage cans," as she described it in her book, *House on Henry Street*. At the end of Ludlow Street, they came to a tenement hallway, went past stinking, uncovered toilets, into a back courtyard where the worst kind of tenements were built. She climbed up muddy steps and finally entered a two-room apartment. There she found a young woman lying in bed in a dark room that opened onto the one other small room. She was covered with dried-up blood from a hemorrhage after giving birth two days before. A family of seven lived in the two rooms, and to pay rent and board, they leased corners of space to other immigrants who slept on makeshift mattresses. The father, a cripple, begged on street corners.

Instead of running from the chaos and foul smells, Miss Wald took over immediately, a nurse on emergency call. As she cleaned up the putrid mess, she comforted the family, assuring them the woman would get well. She washed the patient, and the new baby, and put the fresh sheets she had brought with her on the bed. She washed the other children and scrubbed the floors. After she put the rooms in order, she left them with a promise to return. They kissed her hand in gratitude.

Appalled at the squalor in which decent people were forced to live, emotionally shaken beyond her own capacity to understand what had happened to her, she called this experience her "baptism of fire." Within one half hour everything changed and in her mind her life started anew. All that had happened before she considered irrelevant, unimportant. In effect, she put a flame to the preceding years, obliterating them as effectively as the fire that would destroy her sister Julia's house and with it all her childhood memorabilia.

She had a new vision of herself in which she cared for the sick and worked to change evil social conditions. It seemed to her that this vision sprang whole without previous nurturing. But it capped years of searching: her early dream of helping her brother in a medical practice; leaving home to enter nursing school; her job at the Juvenile Asylum; course work at the Woman's Medical College. She stood at last directed, put together, feeling the power of certainty course through her. Even more energizing than the vision to help others was the realization that she had found a goal. In the debris of poverty she discovered a way to put her skills to use, and above all, she could be herself, a strong, useful woman.

She could relate now only to that urgency. For, she said, "she could not defend herself as part of society that permitted such conditions to exist." And such conditions existed, she said, because people did not know about them. It became her duty, as well as the responsibility of "a citizen in a democracy" to make these flagrant abuses known. It consoled her to think that when the public learned about such horrors, they would be wiped out.

Her naïveté gave her extraordinary strength. She boldly pursued her way, unaware that tenement commissions had investigated and made public the shocking conditions in slum dwellings; that a network of active reformism existed; that young people had already set up settlement houses; that women's groups, missions, churches, and Jewish organizations had invaded the Lower East Side. And what was happening? Nothing. She had yet to learn that it took more than public knowledge to bring about change.

Filled with crusading zeal, she found her studies irrelevant and dropped out of medical college. She recruited to her cause nursing school colleague Mary Brewster who caught Miss Wald's feverish excitement. Together they worked out a plan that had no precedent in nursing. They would live among the poor, share their lives, locate sick people, and nurse them in their own homes.

The courage of their vision made the two young nurses irresistibly winning to the wealthy people they called on for financial support. Even Mr. Jacob Schiff, a tough financier, senior partner in the international banking firm Kuhn, Loeb and Company, could not refuse Miss Wald when she appealed to him through a mutual friend. He wrote to the friend a week later that he intended to be responsible for the nurse's salary. Nor could his mother-in-law, Mrs. Solomon (Betty) Loeb, resist Miss Wald when the nurse called at her town house on East Thirty-eighth Street and, flushed with excitement, poured out her words in her impetuous plea for support. The philanthropic Mrs. Loeb, who entertained lavishly and sponsored the arts, had financed the nursing class that brought Miss Wald to the East Side in the first place. After talking to Miss Wald, she reported to her daughter Nina, "I have had a wonderful experience. I have talked with a young woman who is either crazy or a genius." More impressed with Miss Wald's genius, she too undertook responsibility for a nurse's salary. Between Mr. Schiff and Mrs. Loeb, the two nurses would jointly be guaranteed $120 a month to cover living expenses and nursing supplies. They could request additional funds for special medical needs.

Miss Wald did not realize what a triumph she had scored when she won Jacob Schiff to her side. It was not that wealthy Jews were not charity minded. On the contrary, they considered it a responsibility, and none more so than Mr. Schiff, to care for the needy of their faith. The miracle was that they made room within their system of philanthropy for an unknown such as Lillian Wald. They knew nothing about her or her previous experience. But she won them over. She was passionate, burning with a bright flame, and she combined an irresistible charm with self-confidence.

Braced by the promise of support, the two nurses set out to locate suitable rooms, made difficult by their single requirement that they have "the civilization of a bathroom." They knew that such conveniences were rare but they did not know the hard facts revealed in contemporary reports. Only 306 people out of 255,033 examined had access to bathtubs in their homes. And out of 4,000 tenements that housed 120,000 people, only 51 flats had private toilets.

Two young men, dedicated community workers who lived on Forsyth Street, squired them about one rainy day searching for rooms to rent. Charles B. Stover was a mission worker and theologian, and Edward King, a former journalist, was teaching history to immigrants at the Educational Alliance. When they could not find a decent flat, Stover and King introduced the two nurses to the residents at the College Settlement House on Rivington Street, where head worker Dr. Jane Robbins offered the nurses living quarters.

Settled down among these pioneering women, Miss Wald and Miss Brewster learned they were living with college graduates who had decided to do something concrete about social ills and were sharing the advantages of their education with the unprivileged. They had rented a run-down tenement and converted it into lodgings and meeting rooms for themselves and other residents. When news of their work spread, they received eighty applications within the first year from college women who wanted to join them.

In the exchange of ideas with the settlement house workers, Miss Wald discovered that a new kind of social activism was taking place. The idea of living in the slums had seemed an original one to her, but she found that others had already allied themselves to the slum population. Educated, middle-class people, impelled as much by their need to feel useful as their passion to do good, were experimenting with new forms of organization, founding settlement houses and clubs where they gave classes in English, economics, art, music, and history. Though it had not been part of their original plan, they found themselves immersed in community problems when immigrants turned to them to seek help about housing, jobs, and schools.

The women of the College Settlement and other activists credited their inspiration to Toynbee Hall, the first settlement house in England. In 1884 a group of Oxford and Cambridge students had moved into the most squalid section of the London slums to bring the poor spiritual uplift and to work for reform. They in turn were nourished by the writings of early critics of industrial society such as Thomas Carlyle and John Ruskin. It was Carlyle who claimed that "the liberty to die of starvation is not so divine."

Amherst graduate Stanton Coit brought the settlement idea to the United States and established the Neighborhood Guild in 1886. A year later, Vida Scudder and several other Smith College graduates set up the College Settlement Association, urging women to make their lives meaningful by living and studying among the poor.

The prevailing attitude toward settlement houses was expressed in an article entitled "A Woman's Toynbee Hall" in the magazine *Review of Reviews* of 1890. It described Miss Scudder's project as a way "to render possible for delicately nurtured young women a life of neighborly friendship . . . founded on the belief of the power of friendship to shape character."

And in Chicago, in 1889, Jane Addams and Ella Gates Starr, inspired by Miss Addams's visit to Toynbee Hall a few years before, established Hull House, which became a leading center for social reform. A year later, Charles B. Stover and Edward King took Coit's idea a step further and founded University Settlement in New York City.

Though the burgeoning settlement house movement was a revelation to the two nurses, they did not then see a place for themselves in it. Club work, meetings, education, and self-help groups did not interest them. They remained focused on the immediate and practical matter of finding the sick and nursing them.

Miss Wald and Miss Brewster set out in search of patients within their first few days at the College Settlement House.

4

The Lower East Side

T H E Y were dressed in identical dark blue uniforms with matching hats on their heads. In one hand each clutched a small black bag filled with first-aid equipment such as thermometers, sterile bandages, antiseptics, alcohol, ointments. They threaded their way in and out of pushcarts, through the noise and bustle until they came to Hester Street. There on the dirtiest and most crowded thoroughfare of the East Side, they caught sight of a young boy playing in the litter who had an eye infection they considered so serious that it could result in blindness. They found out his address and set out to locate his flat by knocking at every door in a bulging tenement at 7 Hester Street. As each door opened, they were assailed by the sour odors of rubbish-strewn rooms. They entered each home, gave an impromptu lecture on sanitation, and handed out advice. Where they found infants sick with diarrhea, a fatal malady in the hot summer months, they advised parents to buy uncontaminated milk and demonstrated the rudiments of nursing care. In one flat they arranged for a child with measles to be admitted to a hospital.

The degree to which disease went untreated was shocking to the two nurses. Medical teams sent into the slums by Doctor Blackwell and by Jewish and Christian charities were as useless as a drop of rain on parched earth.

At the end of the day, the nurses wrote up each case for a card file and carefully entered into notebooks every detail of their rounds and expenditures for the monthly report requested by Jacob Schiff. Schiff was a hard taskmaster but the reports had unexpected results. The vivid word pictures Miss Wald drew of the impoverished people in her care involved Schiff further in her work. He became personally interested in the families and asked questions about their welfare to which she would respond in the following report.

In mounting desperation over the extent of the misery they un-covered, the two nurses quickly learned to take advantage of every assistance offered by community charities. One such resource came in the form of tickets for free ice, clothing, and summer excursions which eased marginal lives.

Miss Wald sent Mr. Schiff her first report in the hot summer month of July, 1893.

> Visit and care of typhoid patient 182 Ludlow Street. Visit to 7 Hester Street where in rooms of Nathan Solomon found two chil-dren with measles. After much argument, succeeded in bathing these two patients and the sick baby. The first time in their experience, they insisted, where water and soap could be applied to any one with measles before *seven* days. Brought clean dresses to the older children and gave Herald ice ticket. . . .

> Gave tickets for Hebrew Sanitarium excursion to Mrs. Davis and 3 children, Mrs. Schneider and 5 children . . . but 5 of the children are really naked . . . have no apparel in their possession. So, we will make their decent appearance possible for the picnic. . . .

> In giving tickets for "Hebrew Sanitarium excursion" we find that the people we encounter so wretchedly poor that clothing and car-fare must be provided or the tickets are useless.

> Seven P.M. visit to Mrs. Linowitz, took her flowers, clean bedding, made eggnog and left her in nursing condition for the night. . . .

By August, Schiff agreed that another nurse should be added to the team. The first nurse broke down, Miss Wald informed him, the second stayed only a few days, but the third was now with them. Nevertheless, they were still unable to accomplish their work because they were busy getting relief for "the better class of idle workingmen, who too proud to ask [for] charity, have been virtually starving." She writes:

We have seen among our neighbors many harrowing things, been in the so-called riots and rather resented the incredulous editorials so general in the papers. Almost three weeks ago, I asked the editor of the *Herald* to substitute bread for ice because even then there was nothing to put on the ice. . . .

Many of these people have kept from begging . . . and the pawn-shop tickets tell the progress of their fall . . . All these particulars, you as a philanthropist, are of course acquainted with . . . it is only that one may say, that the tales are general and not at all exceptional that must be peculiar.

Pardon me for entering even thus briefly but we are full of the trouble of our neighbors . . .

Elias Blumenthal living on the Street, only fifteen years old. . . .

Lily Klein very ill with pneumonia . . . the child died but the night before Miss Brewster had remained with the child all night. . . .

Mrs. Jacobson and her two children—homeless, without work . . . Jennie Perk, ill also from organic trouble and poor food. Procured her proper medical treatment. . . .

Samuel Shalinke's wife very ill, whom we nursed but finally induced to go to the hospital, where she died, her baby then was placed at Infant's Hospital . . . and for Samuel himself, work was found by Miss Brewster's people in Pennsylvania.

Mrs. Silverstein, to whom you sent money, is still living . . . but the husband is so worthless and the woman so badly off when we are not there that we are going to persuade her to go to Bellevue and place the children somewhere . . .

In a less morbid tone, she relates the incident of a young Russian student, a "bookworm ambitious to become a good teacher," but who was so destitute, he had no food to eat. But he was also "equally proud," and would not accept help. To get money into his hands, a friend of Miss Wald's pretended her son needed tutoring.

In her August letter, Miss Wald also explained that she and Miss Brewster were looking for a place to live. Their work was not identical to the work of the College Settlement, she wrote, "and now that their regular winter work begins, the rooms that we occupy should be used for workers who give their time wholly to the specific work of the house which as you know is chiefly club work."

She signed her early letters, "Very Earnestly, Lillian D. Wald." She would remain formal in her salutation to her sponsors—"Dear Mr. Schiff and Dear Mrs. Loeb"—was her customary form of address. The endings of her letters softened into "Faithfully yours."

By early September, she informed her sponsors that she and Miss Brewster had a new address—27 Jefferson Street. On the top floor of a six-story tenement walk-up, they had rented a flat of four tiny rooms that was open to sun and light and had a small bathroom in the hallway. They asked the landlord to reduce the nineteen dollars monthly rent, but he argued that "it was a good buy."

They painted the floors, added six-cent white cotton curtains to the windows, and brought in private possessions, simple pieces of furniture, dishes, linens, books, and pictures. Sunlight poured in over growing plants and fresh flowers.

The building janitor, Mrs. McRae, became a treasured friend and protector. From her basement rooms she screened visitors to be sure the two young ladies, living alone in New York, would not be molested nor disturbed when she thought they needed to rest.

To Miss Wald and Miss Brewster, their apartment was simple and cheerful, but to their neighbors, recent arrivals from Russia and Rumania, it was filled with wonderful things. Their first dinner guest, Mrs. McRae's young son Tommy, entranced by the decor and fresh flowers on the table, reported to his mother that the ladies "live like the Queen of England—and eat off solid gold plates."

From this sanctuary the two nurses set out each day, their black bags dangling from their hands. In the two months they had worked out of College Settlement, their preconceptions about the community had undergone change.

To their surprise, they found many in the medical profession hostile to them, viewing a free nursing service as a threat to their incomes. Doctors vied for the hard-earned dollars of the poor. The nurses heard frequent incidents about physicians who demanded money before they would take care of emergencies. This attitude made the immigrant poor terrified of doctors. They equally distrusted the two nurses who, unsummoned, came to their doors and announced they wished to take care of them.

To overcome this aspect of their neighbors' resistance, the nurses became official and pinned silver badges to their hats proclaiming them to be VISITING NURSES UNDER THE AUSPICES OF THE BOARD OF HEALTH. Jacob Schiff intervened to obtain these insignia from the Department of Health; and he also introduced the nurses to a panel of physicians connected to the United Hebrew Charities, men who shared the nurses' concern for the community.

Many years of humiliating experiences had made Miss Wald's neighbors sensitive: They were ashamed to acknowledge certain ailments, such as scabies, as if this skin disease, so easily spread in crowded quarters, marked them with a personal defect. And they dreaded charity, the cold handout that made them feel degraded, and announced a family's inability to sustain itself.

Miss Wald and Miss Brewster hastened to distance themselves from other types of nurses who had made occasional forays to the Lower East Side. The first trained nurses placed in district work had been sent out by the women's branch of the New York City Mission in 1877. Two years later, the Ethical Culture Society placed trained nurses in dispensaries. And fifteen years later, in the 1890s, there were only twenty visiting nurses in the entire country and they were affiliated to churches or charities.

To remove herself from the stigma of charity work, and recognizing her neighbors' needs for dignity and independence, Miss Wald decided to charge a fee for her service. It was only ten cents a visit, but the payment changed the quality of the nurse-patient relationship. Those who could not afford to pay accepted the nurses' care as a friendly act, in the spirit of one neighbor helping another.

Key to Miss Wald's principles was the decision to remain independent and nonsectarian. She and Miss Brewster resisted every effort to have them affiliate with a relief agency. A basic tenet in a democracy, Miss Wald claimed, was that a poor patient had as much right as a wealthy one to call a nurse—and this right existed regardless of racial, religious, or ethnic origin. The nursing service she was building had other unique features: It was headed and administered by nurses themselves; and the nurses lived in the districts in which they worked, thus ensuring a continuing and caring relationship with the patient.

Within a few months, Miss Wald's simple impulse to nurse the poor at their bedside was assuming the characteristics of a "dignified community service," as she called it. She, Miss Brewster, and the growing group of nurses who asked to work with them, educated, healed, and established the basic principles of a Visiting Nurses Service (later called the Visiting Nurse Service).

It did not take long for the community to discover in their midst these two young "ladies who would listen." Neighbors climbed the five flights of stairs and knocked at their door before they set out on their early morning rounds. Such was twenty-one-year-old Samuel, a carpenter and a new bridegroom, pleading that they help his very sick wife. The nurses saw the fright on his face and followed him to his flat on the top floor of a tenement. They found his wife Ida dying from septicemia that had set in after childbirth. The attending midwife explained that a doctor, called in the emergency, had left Ida "lacerated and agonizing" because Samuel could pay only a partial fee. The nurses took Ida to the hospital where she and her baby died a few hours later.

Miss Wald saw thirteen-year-old Louis Rifkin through an open door in a rear tenement flat. His mother, a baby in her arms, was standing over a tub washing butchers' aprons which she did for a living. Why wasn't Louis in school? He had a scaly, sore scalp and the school officials barred him. Louis told them he had never been to school and he felt terrible that at his age he could not read "the names of streets on lamp posts." The dispensaries had not helped him, he complained. Miss Wald examined Louis's scalp and found he had a mild flavus or fungus disease which she cleared up with regular applications of the dispensary ointments. An ecstatic Louis rushed up the five flights of stairs the following semester to tell Miss Wald he was in school and was learning how to read.

Cases piled up. They visited 125 people in January and gave advice to many more who knocked at their door. The disastrous panic of 1893 aggravated grim conditions and the severe economic depression in its wake increased starvation and destitution. Miss Wald watched men leave home mornings and return empty-handed at night, shamefaced, as if unemployment were a personal vice. "The burden of the family is felt in other ways than disease," she wrote to Mr. Schiff, "for work must be procured some way, somehow, and indeed we are not forgetful that means of bringing other relief than healing have been placed in our hands . . . so if we have given to the husband of a patient a ticket to sweep the streets, every hungry man . . . demands like service . . . but it is not adequate and I know that today Miss Brewster and I have seen enough sorrow and poverty and illness to fill a world with sadness . . ."

They bolstered a few lives by handing out work they created: A recent Polish immigrant, a fine seamstress, made Miss Brewster's and Miss Wald's uniforms. Miss Wald sent a young girl whose father was in prison to her sister in Rochester to help in the household; they paid youngsters to run errands.

A litany of tragedy spilled from her pen. "The winter has brought many hard experiences. One not long ago where the baby was born one day and the father shared the bed the next day, complaining of pain which proved to be pneumonia and of which he died. . . . two members at a time of the Davis family, all of whom have typhoid . . ." And then, "Little coffins are stacked mountain high on the deck of the charity commission boat when it makes semi-weekly trips to the cemetery."

As sickness and death swirled out of the stench-filled tenement alleys, she and Miss Brewster began to compile statistics on tuberculosis. Their first expenditures had been for covered sputum cups and carbolic acid disinfectants. Two years later they would turn their list of tubercular patients over to the Board of Health for its campaign against that epidemic disease.

Interspersed in her reports were insights into her neighbors. They are "not being very lovable as a class," she wrote at one point, and "we are always happy to make friends for them," referring to help coming from uptown visitors. At another time she wrote, "We are not discouraged and the more intimately we know these poor Russian Jews, the more frequently are we rewarded with unexpected gleams of attractiveness. Lying is the most frequent vice but affection a more frequent virtue. On my desk now is a bunch of pretty flowers brought today by a Russian for whom we secured work and whose wife we nursed and who is grateful enough to balance a score of ingrates." And then there was the evening the "nice widow and her children took tea with us . . . and tonight some of the neighbors have been calling, and did not leave very early. . . . I mention [this] to show that we have not tired of them, nor they apparently of us."

She was having an unexpected love affair with her neighbors. "You see," she wrote to Mr. Schiff, "I will persist in telling you the nice things of these people. Miss Brewster does not lag in seeing the good some do possess or in being their apologist either. I always feel that it must be a pleasure to know this."

She remarked on the vigor and determination of immigrants, streaming in daily to the Lower East Side from Ellis Island. Despite poverty's crippling effects, they survived. They bonded together into religious and kinship groups, and families clung together in smothering closeness, as if that would ward off evil. Some found the burdens of poverty weightless against the promise of life in the new world. Jews, who made up 90 to 95 percent of the Lower East Side population, no longer condemned to a ghetto, studied English and drummed into their children the need for an education. Others drew strength from the patterns of religious rituals, such as the family Miss Wald visited one Sabbath eve. With no money to buy food, pots filled with water instead of the usual broth bubbled on the stove.

When people could find work, their lives were degraded by long hours and filthy conditions. They sweated out their labor in broken-down neighborhood factories or in their own homes where whole families, including youngsters from ages six to twelve, worked fourteen hours a day wrapping cigars, making artificial flowers, or trimming clothes.

Radicals of all persuasions discussed poverty and revolution while sitting over glasses of tea in the cafés on Suffolk Street. Miss Wald had no time to join them but their heated debates and militant spirit pervaded the neighborhood. She met German socialists, Italian revolutionaries, Marxists, anarchists, and single taxers, but she did not understand their political talk. Nor was she ready for the trade union meetings taking place in the community. But she did laugh and cry at the plays presented at Yiddish theaters, considered the most vital in New York. And she read Morris Rosenfeld's stirring poetry about immigrant life.

The raw turmoil of human emotion in the tenement world drew uptown writers seeking local color and access to its vitality. An aspiring writer, Ernest Poole, came from Princeton to write short stories about broken, squalid lives. He found residence at the University Settlement and wrote instead tracts about the painful sight of tubercular children "coughing out their lungs." Harvard-educated Hutchins Hapgood reported on the vigorous talents of actors, writers, and artists like the young, struggling Jacob Epstein, who lived and worked in a one-room studio on Hester Street. Lincoln Steffens, learning from Jacob A. Riis how to be a police reporter, began to study immigrant conditions and stored away in his memory scenes of police clubbing strikers, and young prostitutes taking over the streets. Others pointed to the dramatic clash between the aged and the young: Old Testament figures, slight men in large black hats and long black coats, curls growing down the sides of their faces, alongside brazen, aggressive youth flaunting an Americanized life-style.

Lillian Wald and Mary Brewster were engulfed in this tumultuous world. They worked without surcease, climbing up and down hundreds of flights of stairs, scrambling over connecting rooftops to save time and energy. They rushed patients to the hospital or assisted with surgery in the home, nursing their patients, succoring them, loving them, and in no way able to meet the deluge of cases.

An exhausted Miss Wald wrote her reports to Mr. Schiff each month. Bitter cold in the winter, she wrapped herself in blankets, put her feet in the oven, and meticulously listed comments and expenditures.

Miss Brewster broke down under the strain. In the crisis, Mrs. McRae spelled Miss Wald at Miss Brewster's bedside. She had been completely won over by the gentle, sweet nurse, her favorite of the two women. Only Miss Wald's insistence that Mrs. McRae get some rest forced her from the top floor flat. One morning, on opening her door, Miss Wald found her neighbor curled up in the hallway, fast asleep.

When Miss Brewster was taken to the hospital, the neighbors had to be restrained from flocking there to show "their affectionate concern." Touched by their loyalty, Miss Wald let Mr. Schiff know how loving they were. But Mr. Schiff was equally concerned over Miss Brewster. In the fall of 1894 when it looked as if she might be able to return to work, he sent her a note. "Nothing would give me greater pleasure," he wrote, "than if you find yourself in a position to give the great cause in which you and Miss Wald labor your continued cooperation. . . . Rest assured that this is great encouragement to me personally."

The extent to which Lillian Wald had shaped a new set of values was made evident by her response to news from home. She expressed her sympathies to the family on the death of her Uncle Morris, but she had a different view of his business reversals. Barely three years before she would have fully shared his anger when the United Garment Workers of America tried to organize his shop. Rather than accede to trade union demands, he had temporarily shut down his business. At his death in 1894, the economic slump and changing work conditions forced his firm into bankruptcy. All his assets were assigned to creditors. Her Uncle Henry, too, was forced to shut down his business and declare a moratorium on the payment of judgments to creditors.

A style of life was collapsing. And Miss Wald was identifying with progressive forces she had never perceived in Rochester. Her sensibilities had sharpened on the Lower East Side and she could hear the desperate cries for change. They came out of the neighborhood of which she was now a part and in which she would continue to define herself.

Her tiny apartment had become a magnet not only for those seeking nursing care but for social reformers and wealthy uptown people of the Schiff-Loeb circle who admired her pioneer work and wanted to become part of it.

Among those who climbed the stairs was Josephine Shaw Lowell, a community leader and founder of the Consumers League of New York. Mrs. Lowell had turned her back on organized charity when she learned of its link to politics. In the same forthright way, she recognized that the problems of poverty and unemployment had to be tackled *before* people became public charges. She wrote to her sister, "It is better to save them [people] before they go under than to spend your life fishing them out when they're half drowned and taking care of them afterwards."

In the winter of 1893, Mrs. Lowell offered to run errands and do other menial chores to save Miss Wald's energy for nursing. Not only was she a genius in community activity, Miss Wald realized, but also in attracting new workers. Though Miss Wald was inexperienced, especially in handling the complicated problems brought on by the severe economic depression, Mrs. Lowell nevertheless made a comrade of the obscure nurse, asking her to cosign letters to the press, and gradually involving her in larger community issues. "I could see even then that she meant to have me feel the importance of serving the neighborhood," Miss Wald would say at a later date.

In observing Mrs. Lowell at work, Miss Wald learned how to make better use of her own time and energy. And she took her first step beyond nursing when she joined Mrs. Lowell in the Lower East Side Relief, an organization to provide work for the unemployed.

Still, she felt like a neophyte when she was invited to join the prestigious Social Reform Club in 1894. Its distinguished membership of professionals, intellectuals, labor leaders, and selected workers was dedicated to social change. She learned about the philosophy of Tolstoy from Ernest Crosby, a Tolstoy disciple and first president of the club, who would become one of her most enthusiastic supporters. She met Mary Simkhovitch, founder of Greenwich House; Charles B. Spahr of *Outlook* magazine; Professor Felix Adler, head of the Ethical Culture Society; and another newcomer, frail, slender Leonora O'Reilly, the only woman worker in the group. She listened to eloquent debates on how to change the world by her old friends Charles Stover and Edward King; and talked with her sponsor Jacob Schiff and his wife who occasionally attended meetings.

At about the same time she became acquainted with Jacob A. Riis, then a police reporter beginning to battle the slums, and his friend Theodore Roosevelt, in his early career as New York City Police Commissioner.

Miss Wald had worked out a simple plan for nursing the sick in an economically depressed community. In doing so she had touched a nerve at a time when dynamic forces for change were erupting, and she became the focus for ideas and activism she never knew existed. She felt people tugging at her, wanting her to become more than she meant to be. They saw the dimensions of her skill and personality. And she herself realized that the poor needed help, not only when sick, but with grave problems they barely understood.

If she was to become involved in community work, she could not also run up and down tenement stairs, nurse the sick, clean the floors, and take patients to the hospital. She was "driven" ("we were driven to everything we did," she would say) to look for larger quarters. In April, 1895, Jacob Schiff bought a house on Henry Street and arranged for its repair and furnishing. She knew she had become more than a nurse.

Lillian Wald's mother, Minnie Wald

Her father, Max D. Wald

"Favey," her maternal grandfather

Rabbi Max Landsberg of the Reform Jewish
Congregation, Rochester, New York

Lillian D. Wald, a nurse in training

Class of 1891, School of Nursing, New York Hospital. Lillian Wald is seated to the left of Irene Sutliffe, who is dressed in black and holding the infant. Mary Brewster is standing in back of and to the right of Miss Sutliffe. The infant was a foundling raised by the nurses and finally adopted by Miss Sutliffe.

An ambulance of the 1890s

Dr. Elizabeth Blackwell

Hester Street pushcart market, 1898

Five Cents A Spot. Lodgers crowded into a Bayard Street tenement, c. 1889

EXPENDITURES

January 1895

Carfare .20 Eggs for Mrs. Dorfman .25	.45
Mrs. Kirchbaum to buy potatoes which she peddled and made money and has not returned for aid or received it from the U.H.C.	3.00
Eggs for Mrs. Klein .25 Milk bill paid at Lee-To-Lum for	.25
Dorfman .30; Rich .82; Matlin .84; Sinavoy .96; Chwech .64; Newman .82	3.96
Two prescriptions Mrs Klein .40 grapes for Sweeney girls .25	.65
Carfare .10 Messenger .10	.20
Jennie Ramber to Saranac expenses	30.00
Schnitteman carfare to hospital .10 – 10 for the trip	.20
Rettig coal .25 Messenger .10	.35
Dorsky medicine .25 carfare .20 Schnitteman medicine .25	.70
Miss Loeb's carfare ten weeks	1.95
	41.71
Dorsky food .25	.25
Carfare .20 Messenger .20	.40
Sinavoy eggs .25. Kreiss medicines .20 Schnitteman eggs .10	.55
McCrea medicines .20	.20
Moshkovich provisions .25 Chwech provisions .25 Casper medicine .40	.90
Manheim medicine .20 carfare .25 Klein chicken .76	1.21
Sinavoy eggs .07 Brown eggs .15. carfare .10	.32
Holtzer milk .06 Long medicines .30 Stamps 2.00	2.36
Telephone U.H.C. .15 Charmarck medicines .20	.35
Carfare .10 Klein .06 Mrs. Faber towards rent 3.00	3.16
Milk bill at Lee-Te-Lum ; Dorfman .12 Kreiss .42 Klein .60	
Chwech .54 Sinavoy .54 Lieberman .60 Matlin .54	3.36
Rafter eggs .10 Klein chicken .48 Messenger .20	.78
Chwech baby at Day Nursery 90 Sheriff .25	.25
	14.09
Rettig two prescriptions .40 Mrs. Miller medicine .20	.60
Telephone N.Y. Hospital .15 Mrs Chwech to hospital .30	.45
Medicine Manheim .20 carfare .15 messenger .10 (100)	.45
Sinavoy provisions .36 Marcusen A.S.B. tablets .35	.71
Chwech to Bellevue .25	.25
Messenger .10 Lipske fixing spectacles .18	.28
Chwech provisions .40	.40
Two prescriptions Mrs. Klein .40 Sweeney fruit .30	.70
Kimmil .05 Mara food .20 Telephone Mt. Sinai Hospital .16	.40
Klein eggs .25 Chwech food .50 Berger eggs .05	.80
Klein .10 Messenger .25 fare .10 eggs .25 P.cards 1.00	
Messenger .15	1.85
Diamond medicines .20	.20
Stationery 1.00 messenger for Mary Wenzell .20 for soup .10	1.30
Messenger hospital for Mary Wenzell .25 carfare .15	.40
Mrs. Lichterman's rent	7.00
	$75.99

Monthly expenditures

Lillian Wald and Mary Brewster in their office at 265 Henry Street, 1895

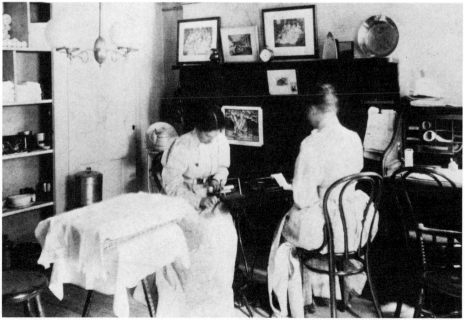

A Visiting Nurse climbing over a rooftop

The "Family," about 1900. Seated, left to right: Mary Magoun Brown, Lavinia Dock, Lillian Wald, Ysabella Waters, Henrietta Van Cleft. Standing, left to right: Jane Hitchcock, Sue Foote, Jeanne Travis. In front, two Henry Street children, Sammie Brofsky and Florrie Long

5

The House
She Lived In

F R O M the beginning she had a sense of belonging to 265
Henry Street. It would be a center for the Visiting Nurses Service, and it would also be her home. From a small rented office next
door at the Louis Technical School, where she had taught hygiene to
a group of immigrant women two years before, she supervised repairs. Workmen restored the gleam to hardwood floors, mahogany
doors, and hand-carved moldings, and when fireplaces were put into
working order, and brass doorknobs and fixtures polished, she made
plans to move in.

The simple red brick building, Georgian in style of architecture,
was set in a row of similar houses, each with a small backyard. It
was a relic of the 1830s when lower Manhattan was still fashionable.
Decay had set in as the flood of immigration made real estate a
profitable business and drove the middle class uptown. Landlords
converted private homes into multiple dwellings, built tenements in
the narrow streets, charged high rents, reduced maintenance, and
brought about the wretched living conditions with which Miss Wald
was so familiar.

Somehow Henry Street had escaped the blight of six-floor, "dumbbell" tenements as they were called and, once moved in, Miss Wald could look out her windows in the evening into the distant glow of the sunset on the Williamsburgh suspension bridge that spanned the East River between Manhattan and Brooklyn.

There was romance to the neighborhood and she made scraps of its historic legacy her own. She would tell visitors that the American Revolutionary soldier, Nathan Hale, was picked up by the British as a spy and hanged without a trial a few blocks away in the Rutgers's orchard. A nearby church still had a slave gallery, and two doors down was New York's first fire station, installed by Tammany Boss Tweed.

By the time she took over the house in the summer of 1895, she knew that the number of nurses asking to work with her and become residents would overflow the rooms. Some years later, 267 Henry Street was acquired and the walls broken through to connect the two buildings. From the outside the houses maintained their spare, lean look but their interiors were redesigned to house the growing "family."

In Miss Wald's master plan for the house, nurse residents took over small bedrooms on the top floor with a single hallway bathroom. Below that she created her private space, converting the pillared balcony off her bedroom into a sleeping porch. On the same floor she had her office and a living room she decorated with possessions reminiscent of her family's Victorian homes—a Persian rug, a grand piano, damask chairs and sofas, fringed lamps and pictures. A clutter of framed snapshots of family and friends would cover every tabletop.

The dining room on the floor below became the meeting room for residents and guests. Here too she gave it the look of a private home, enriched years later by gifts of antiques from friends, a Duncan Phyfe dining table, silver tea service, and silver candelabra on mahogany buffets. She added old and new pieces of copper and brass she bought from a nearby tradesman whose shop became a favorite haunt for her and her friends.

On the ground floor, often called the basement, were the clinic rooms and offices that Lillian Wald and Mary Brewster set up. (For a brief period Miss Brewster made the transition to Henry Street but ill health soon forced her to retire from her profession.) As announced in the spring issue of *Outlook*, "the house will have a bathroom which will be used for emergencies and for the bathing of children before they are sent to the country."

She moved into Henry Street hardly aware of the impact she would make on the community. Her unique requirement that nurses live in the neighborhood they serve turned the house into an immediate sanctuary for sick and needy neighbors who found not only nursing care but friends and confidantes.

A band of pioneer nurses shared her excitement about the exceptional approach to their profession. Among the first to join her was Lavinia Lloyd Dock, described by a colleague as a "small, short, sort of roly poly little person with curly hair." Nothing in Lavinia Dock's indifferent looks revealed the depth of her understanding nor the passion of her political commitment. She became one of Miss Wald's most important friends.

The two women had in common a middle-class background and private school education. But the adventurous Miss Dock had gone into disaster relief after graduation from the Bellevue Hospital School of Nursing, aiding victims of the Johnstown Flood at one time; at another, the sick and dying in a yellow fever epidemic. She had been a district nurse in the New York City Mission; an assistant head of the Johns Hopkins School of Nursing for five years; and was the author of *Materia Medica*, one of the first nursing textbooks. While at Henry Street, she and colleague Adelaide Nutting would co-author a four-volume history of nursing.

Nursing was Miss Dock's profession but she preferred talking about suffrage for women. One evening, coming directly from a suffrage meeting to the Columbia School of Nursing to give a lecture, she walked in with banners plastered on her hat and chest reading "Votes for Women."

"What can you expect from men," she wrote to Miss Wald in 1903, after Seth Low, liberal mayor of New York, was defeated in the election. "It destroys one's faith in the possibility of their [men's] doing any better. Is there any hope for the future?" she asked. "O I could sit down and weep over it all." She advised Miss Wald to devote herself to the extension of nursing, to rest. "Women," she said, "do the scullery work, then men take over."

Convinced that suffrage for women would bring about a more equable society, she persuasively argued about it, as well as about socialism and pacifism. In 1907 she joined a militant faction of the suffrage movement that brought the struggle to·people on the streets and into factories, and organized the first Fifth Avenue suffrage parades. Miss Wald would be found in the line of march along with an impressive showing of nurses in blue uniforms.

In the give and take of working at Henry Street, Miss Dock also won advantages. "It was at Henry Street that I really began to think," she said, for she had the privilege of working with Miss Wald, "a social genius, the fortunate possessor of a touchstone which reveals to her the best and finest possibilities of the natures about her ... the gift for bringing people and opportunities ... together."

Miss Dock quietly went about the business of founding an international nursing association, writing books, editing the foreign section of the *American Journal of Nursing*. Not only a militant suffragist, she was a linguist, musician, scholar, and pacifist. Still, word was out, "You must not praise her. She does not like it." Shy of the spotlight, she did her daily stint making nursing rounds and putting her penetrating insights at the service of Henry Street. As much as anyone, she helped Lillian Wald give shape to the profession of public health nursing, putting her scholarship into many of Miss Wald's speeches and articles.

In residence at Henry Street along with Miss Dock were Ysabella G. Waters, an 1897 graduate of the Johns Hopkins School of Nursing, Harriet Knight, another trained nurse, and Anne W. Goodrich, Miss Wald's colleague from the New York School of Nursing. Miss Goodrich became staff coordinator and also lectured at the Columbia School of Nursing where Adelaide Nutting headed the department. Among the residents was the first member of the laity, as nonprofessionals were called. Helen McDowell, daughter of a famous Civil War general, was a generous, warmhearted woman with a special talent for working with children, who called her "Tante Helene." She bought a house facing the rear of Henry Street and opened it up for special children's programs in music and theater.

Others—Lina Rogers, Roberta Shatz, Elizabeth Farrell, Mary Magoun Brown, and Jane Hitchcock—would become important members of the nursing staff. Miss Wald raised money for their work from generous friends, notably the Schiffs, the Paul Warburgs, the Felix Warburgs, Leonard Lewisohn, John Crosby, and others. In the early years, nurses' salaries were often paid through individual grants such as one provided by Henry Morgenthau who supported a nurse for twenty-two years. Organizations also used this method to fund nurses' salaries, among them the Ethical Culture Society and the Directors of the Presbyterian Hospital. Miss Georgia Beaver, the fourth nurse to join Henry Street, was supported through the Ethical Culture Society for the seven years she was on the staff. She thought of Miss Wald as a beautiful person, a charming, vivid creature who was a genius even in the first years. "She introduced a home atmosphere into the nucleus of the Henry Street Settlement," she said, with the "subtle touch of an artist in her work," creating a warm, friendly atmosphere, and "blessed with generous friends."

This group of women, educated, middle class, and unmarried, became Lillian Wald's "family," and the center of her life at Henry Street. When in 1900 the number of residents grew to fifteen, the first few nested into an inner circle, or her "steadies" and provided a continuous network of support. With them Miss Wald shared the same direction and interests, and found a haven of safety where her emotional needs were quickly understood. They, in turn, cared deeply for their head resident whose ingenuity had created a unique living and working space, and whose vision gave them opportunities for professional growth. Henry Street rang with their high spirits, their laughter at each other's foibles, and with their frank talk in criticism and friendship. Without ties to husbands and children, thus freed from family chores and domestic conflicts, they gave their creative minds completely to their work. Imaginative programs proliferated out of Henry Street with the abundance of a harvest.

Lillian Wald, centered and supported within the house, became the public figure, the face that represented Henry Street. She was the visionary; she had the executive ability and the personality to ally Henry Street with the larger world—to financial supporters, to related movements, to the march of people pressing government to assume responsibility for public welfare.

Mornings at 7:30 Miss Wald met with her staff around the breakfast table, perhaps the only time they gathered together. Seated at the head of the table with a basket of mail and messages, she discussed requests for nurses from individuals, physicians, and dispensaries. "Please send a nurse to me to tell me how to bring up my baby. She is my first," was a typical note. Often Miss Wald distributed tickets for concerts and plays sent in by friends.

After breakfast, nurses filed out of Henry Street on their rounds, dressed alike in blue uniforms and matching hats, carrying the now famous black bags. They walked through familiar, pushcart-laden streets and winding alleys, making house calls.

Under Miss Wald's guidance, they became completely involved with their patients and with the community, linking health to home conditions, sanitation, food, employment, and mental and emotional stress. A nurse might recommend a job for an unemployed husband, or a change in jobs; look into a child's problems at school or with the police; often they dipped into their purses to supply money for food and rent.

In the process of developing community health care, Miss Wald established the early concepts of preventive medicine and the treatment of the whole patient. Her nurses became guardians of public health. They fanned out to thousands of tenement families who paid the nominal ten- to twenty-five-cent fee, if they could, and for the first time in their lives had personal health care. Heretofore, they waited until critical illness forced them to dispensaries or the hospital. Miss Wald was adamant about treating the sick in their homes. It kept the family together, she said, in itself an important lift to the spirits. The records of active and dismissed cases maintained by Miss Wald's nurses showed a better statistical record for recovery when compared to similar hospital cases.

The "noices," as the children called them, were becoming a treasured feature of the neighborhood. They could walk unmolested through wretched streets, known centers of violence and vice. Heedless of danger, a nurse would respond to a tap on an apartment window beckoning her in to take care of a man's leg ailment or a sick child. And Miss Wald herself, the head resident, was beginning to assume the misty outlines of a ministering angel.

She was deeply involved in the neighborhood, making changes, projecting new programs when, in the fall of 1898, Jane Addams, leader of the best-known settlement in the country, Hull House of Chicago, came for her first visit and sat next to Miss Wald at the breakfast table.

The two women made an astonishing contrast in appearance and personality. The fair-skinned, blue-eyed Miss Addams, her light brown hair drawn simply back into a knot, looked out at the world with a direct and steady gaze. She was settled in appearance, serene in manner, and wise as if her keen eyes had surveyed and her mind had cataloged all the known ills of industrial society. Next to her, Miss Wald's spirit seemed untried, restless with energy. She had not had Miss Addams's intellectual training but her mind was quick. She could size up a situation in a flash and know what had to be done and how to do it. She was imaginative, creative, decisive. From the particular she arrived at a universal truth. Miss Addams seemed by comparison low in physical vitality. She had harnessed her energy to her mind, a powerful, perceptive instrument. Every thought she expressed was freshly minted, lucid. In writings that have become classics, she gave the settlement house movement its philosophic underpinnings.

Miss Addams contended that reform work, objectively desirable for the improvement of social conditions, also had subjective rewards. Drawing on her own feelings of uselessness as a middle-class woman, and the empty future she faced after college, she fostered settlement house work as an outlet for educated women who did not know how to utilize their skills. She insisted that the productive labor of a settlement house would make them feel vital and important.

Neither woman challenged men's political domination. Men could vote and men held office. Nonetheless, compelled by their vision of a just society, they became visible and powerful on behalf of their unprivileged constituents. They could do so only with the support of the settlement houses and organizations for which they spoke. Both natural leaders, Miss Wald and Miss Addams, along with many others initiated reforms that would give a different shape to industrial society.

Meeting at the breakfast table at Henry Street, the two women not only had similar concerns for human welfare, but touched each other along a deep inner core, as if they shared a special nuance of language. Both women found their support in networks of women and understood the dynamics of different life-styles.

At this first meeting, Miss Wald was breathless in her admiration, pleased that Miss Addams approved of her work. She wrote to Miss Addams afterward that she struggled "between a longing to weep and a longing to say in more articulate language . . . how much, how very much realizing you is to me." At another time she wrote, "Beloved Lady . . . I long to see you and refresh my soul with your wisdom."

They addressed each other in the style of the day as "Dearest Lady," or "Beloved Lady," or perhaps only "Lady," a common form of salutation for the upper class that was graced with affection, yet evoked the formality of Victorian society when first names were not in popular use. In the circles in which Miss Addams and Miss Wald moved, each was also referred to as "Leading Lady."

Soon after Miss Addams's visit, one of Hull House's most forceful residents moved to Henry Street. In 1899, Mrs. Florence Kelley left Jane Addams's inner circle and joined Miss Wald's, when she arrived in New York to become general secretary of the Consumers League. Here was a woman so mercilessly bright, remarked Miss Wald, that she could be brilliant even at breakfast.

Mrs. Kelley was a large, handsome woman with firm features, wide mouth and dark, thick hair braided around her head. She was always theatrically dressed in black, "without stays," commented a contemporary. Her mind, able to hold facts and figures about factory conditions, made her a formidable opponent. Miss Wald chuckled in relating an incident at a conference on factory conditions which she attended with Mrs. Kelley. She overheard one employer say to another, "You know this bill is all wrong, why don't you say something?" To which the other replied, "What, and let that fire-eater in the black dress make a monkey of me?"

Married and divorced, the mother of three children who were often cared for by friends, she was a lawyer and social activist. While studying abroad after graduation from Cornell University, she became a friend of the socialist Friedrich Engels, and translated and published in the United States one of his books and a work by Karl Marx. She was also the author of a significant early treatise, *Our Toiling Children*, and had held a top position in the state of Illinois as special investigator of child labor conditions. No aspect of the political process was alien to her, for her father, after nine years as a Philadelphia judge, had been elected to Congress, where for twenty years he served on the powerful Ways and Means Committee.

In her new position as head of the Consumers League, Mrs. Kelley toured the country to speak at every gathering no matter how small, at colleges, unions, civic centers—as well as before legislative committees—to urge people into action and teach them how to pressure big business to improve working conditions. She made the organization national in scope by adding sixty chapters, and called international conferences.

Mornings at Henry Street were spiced by her relentless wit at Miss Wald's breakfast table. A newspaper in her hand, she would make cutting remarks about headline stories of trivial matters while issues of human concern went unreported. Miss Wald herself was the butt of her scorn on one occasion when the head resident defended a woman by remarking, "Well, she has an open mind," to which Mrs. Kelley retorted, "That's what I object to. It's open top and bottom."

Mrs. Kelley was the "sun and the wind and she practically demolished her opponents," said Henry Street volunteer Rita Wallach Morgenthau in a radio address some years later. Miss Wald, on the other hand, won her points by "her forbearance and understanding her opponents."

The two women were different only in manner. Fundamentally they were allies in the fight for social change, especially for children. Miss Wald welcomed Mrs. Kelley to Henry Street as a member of the laity. And to Mrs. Kelley, who had trying moments of solitude and despair, Miss Wald's warmth was vital: "Your loving kindness made the difference between my feeling an exile and feeling myself within a circle of interest and affection . . ." When Mrs. Kelley's daughter, who was attending an out-of-town college, suddenly died, Miss Wald solaced the grieving mother by accompanying her to a mountain retreat.

The powerful political minds of Lavinia Dock, Florence Kelley, and, on her frequent visits, Jane Addams acted like strong currents around Miss Wald. Her own perceptions of the connection between health and economic and social conditions had forced her into social activism. But the insights of the political members of her "family" opened her eyes to the entrenched disparities between rich and poor and the need for political solutions. Nevertheless, she drew from her friends only what she thought feasible, practical. She had her own individual strength—decisiveness, understanding, and charm that drew people like a magnet. "All the world would come sooner or later to her door," said Mrs. Kelley. "They came from Downtown and Uptown Manhattan, and from every country on earth," wrote the social activist Josephine Goldmark. People felt secure within her embrace. She cast her warmth over the community, creating a flow of trust between nurses and neighbors.

If neighbors saw Miss Wald and Henry Street as a sanctuary, she saw them as individuals—complex, culturally varied, yet pulling together. She listened to them and what they said helped form her programs.

6

Endangered
Children

"T H I S must be like the scenes of country life in English novels," commented a neighborhood young man when he saw the playground Miss Wald had created by combining Henry Street's small backyard with two adjoining ones. In the enlarged space an old wisteria vine on a trellis formed an arbor covering most of one wall. Two ailanthus trees, scorned in fancy neighborhoods as weeds, hung their green branches over another fence. In window boxes and flower beds plants were in bloom.

Safe, bright, clean, cheerful space—this first playground on the Lower East Side marked a new era. Residents lined up to get in to the "Bunker Hill" of playgrounds, as it was called, after the first battle of the American Revolution.

Miss Wald had originally planned to put the backyard to use for "cripples, chronic invalids and convalescents," she explained to an interviewer for *Outlook* magazine in May. But she learned that a safe play area was also needed for healthy youngsters when parents complained that their children were injured by wagons and carriages while playing in congested streets. And she saw children at their outdoor games dodging traffic and so transformed the backyard into play space for the healthy and the sick, for the young and old.

The popularity of the playground forced her to allocate specific hours for each group. Mornings found toddlers and preschool children of working mothers playing in a sandbox under a striped awning. In the afternoons, school children swung along parallel bars and climbed ladders. Summer evenings resounded with the songs and dances of workers for whom it became a social gathering place. Fathers and mothers took their babies there on warm weekends, sat in patches of shade under the arbor, and drank tea or lemonade.

Children were under Lillian Wald's eye all the time—hundreds and hundreds of them playing in crowded streets, attending crowded schools, living in crowded homes. They were stalked by hunger, disease, and fear, locked into a seamless pocket of poverty. Didn't Nature intend all children to have a fair share in life? she asked.

In their earliest days on Jefferson Street, she and Mary Brewster had automatically placed emphasis on educating expectant mothers in prenatal care, on training women about proper feeding of the newborn, on the teaching of hygiene and simple procedures for the care of the sick child. They urged the city to cut down on infant mortality by providing stations for the purchase of uncontaminated milk. What was the point in helping in the birth of a child, she asked, if she did not help that child grow?

Growing also meant a touch of beauty. At the height of the 1893 panic, Miss Wald had written to Mr. Schiff, "It is a matter of regret to Miss Brewster and me that . . . we cannot do enough for them [after] having parted from the sick bed . . . occasionally [we] invite some for a meal. As soon as we have time we intend to take a small party of the brightest young ones to the park and the museums."

She became the central figure in mobilizing the Lower East Side behind a petition campaign urging the Metropolitan Museum of Art to remain open on Sundays so that working people and their children could view exhibitions. The museum would subsequently report that on Sundays, "the laboring classes were well represented."

She was burdened by the need to spread the word, to arouse government and public to the fate of children who were being irreparably damaged. Surely the rich were not so frozen into their class position, so greedy for riches, that they were indifferent to the needs of millions living in the slums? she asked. She became a publicist on behalf of children, joining with new social forces to awaken social conscience to their condition. Through years of work, she cajoled, pressured, persuaded, and ultimately helped create an educated, concerned body of opinion.

While clubs, classes, lectures, and other programs were developing within Henry Street, she was moving out into the public arena. In 1898, she helped form the Outdoor Recreation League which obtained land from the city for a neighborhood park. Florence Kelley took a dim view of city parks when she saw real estate operators build tall tenements opposite the cleared space and clog the neighborhood more than ever with residents. "There are too many people for the streets," Mrs. Kelley complained. But to Miss Wald each playground and park—Columbus Park, created out of a slum called Mulberry Bend, Hamilton Fish, and others—were victories. At her urging, public schools stayed open after school and during summers to serve as recreation centers, for which she became a volunteer inspector. By 1902, a liberal city administration under Mayor Seth Low appropriated money and equipment for New York City's first municipal playground, Seward Park.

She asked wealthy uptown supporters to open their country homes to neighborhood children. Day excursions and weekend visits expanded into week-long visits, and finally to the establishment of Henry Street camps when friends bequeathed their estates to the settlement. In this way Riverholm on the Hudson River came into existence, and Camp Henry, House in the Woods, and Echo Hill Farm. By 1899, Henry Street established the first convalescent home for women, children, and workers.

The sight of Lower East Side children running in a field of flowers, over a country trail, or romping in the sun at the seashore renewed her faith and energy.

One of these youngsters was eight-year-old Charles Guttman, who lived near the settlement at 301 Henry Street. In adulthood, Mr. Guttman contributed $500,000 to the Henry Street Settlement

House. He explained the reasons for his gift to an interviewer. "The Henry Street Settlement House took me and a lot of Irish and Italian kids and sent us off to the country," he said. "You can't explain what a thrill it was. I'll never forget it . . . and there's no way I can really pay them back. I never knew what a cow was. Sure, I knew what grass was, and goats, we had plenty of that in those days in the East 70s and 80s. But a cow? No, sir."

"This contribution," continued Mr. Guttman, "doesn't even the score, but at least it serves to mark an experience that helped open a poor boy's eyes to the possibilities of life in America."

Miss Wald's personal touch was everywhere, arranging flowers in a room, or bringing bright toys into the kindergarten. Her instinctive response to children's needs opened other doors for them. On the complaint of a young boy that "I can never study at home because [my] sister is always using the table," she allocated rooms at Henry Street for study halls and provided tutors. She took the idea further, pressuring the Board of Education to maintain study rooms in schools. She worked with school teacher Elizabeth Farrell who urged special classes for special children. By 1900, the Board of Education permitted Miss Farrell to form the first ungraded classroom for the physically handicapped and for those with learning disabilities.

Miss Wald's concern over the health situation in schools resulted in the hiring of the first public school nurse. She knew that seriously ill children were at school spreading contagious diseases while children with minor ailments, such as eczema, were playing on the streets, truants from the classroom. To convince the School Board that a nurse *in* school could set the situation right, she offered to pay half the salary of Henry Street nurse Lina Rogers if the Board of Education paid the other half. Miss Rogers supervised four schools, examining sick children in school, identifying their illnesses, consulting with the school physician, and visiting the sick children in their homes. Naturally, the schools under Miss Roger's supervision showed better attendance and healthier children. It was common sense to Miss Wald that a skilled nurse in every school would achieve the same results. The Board of Education reluctantly agreed and made school nurses part of the sytsem.

Each step led to another. Thus school nurses, on spontaneous visits to homes, established connections between families and Miss Wald. They reported to her that they often found a sick child sharing a bed in a dark and airless room with five or six others; that children were often abused; and that many children had either no breakfasts or only poor ones left for them by working parents who ran off to jobs or who were ignorant about nutrition. Children therefore came to school undernourished, if not actually hungry.

The hard facts of poverty breeding illness, and the interaction of environment, nutrition, and health were like the tangled vines in a jungle through which she had to cut her way. To feed the children properly, she urged that schools provide lunches. Why the fuss over such a program? she wanted to know, when confronted with the usual bureaucratic opposition. Such programs were popular in Europe, and in private schools in the United States. Surely less privileged children should be fed, not as a charity but as their right, as a simple human measure. Undernourished children cannot learn their lessons in school, she said. They often appear mentally defective when they are simply hungry. Working with others waging the same battle, she achieved another victory when school lunches were introduced into the system.

The schools were so overcrowded that "Compulsory education is a farce in this vicinity," she wrote to Jacob Schiff in 1894. "Many children cannot be placed even when schools divide classes into half days." The *New York Times* let the public know that the "Head worker of Henry Street Settlement opposes shorter school days." Families agreed with Miss Wald on the need for full school days as insuring "a safe refuge under skilled care of teachers." City life was too difficult for children, Miss Wald maintained, and part days in school provided inadequate protection from the dangers of the city streets. She saw too many youngsters hanging around poolrooms, joining street gangs, turning to violence and crime. She saw too many young women of school age, "unfortunate creatures," she

called them, hanging around doorways, earning money as prostitutes.

Court records showed that children of newly arrived immigrants
outnumbered the native born in court cases by three and a half to
one because "home life was so unbearable." What will happen to the
country if these children can't assume responsibilities in a democracy, she asked. "As a nation we must rise or fall as we serve or fail
these future citizens."

Nothing drove her so incessantly as the sight of children put to
work, both on the streets and in the home. Some were sent out by
their parents to earn a a few pennies before and after school. She saw
them in ragged clothes, shivering on cold days, selling newspapers,
hawking wares, polishing shoes. At home, many started work at six
and seven years of age, often in a single room jammed with a dozen
people, including their mothers and fathers. In some flats kitchens
and bedrooms were converted to home factories. They lost their
childhoods in labor, working half the night, breathing foul air in
windowless rooms, eating rotting food. Tenement labor was on the
increase in the early 1900s, creating physically and mentally stunted
children, victims of eye disease, tuberculosis, and early death. Scenes
haunted Miss Wald's waking hours and disturbed her sleep: Fran-
cesca sewing buttons on coats; Santa picking out nut meats; Tiffy
helping her mother at finishing clothes; Giuseppe working on artificial flowers. One of her nurses reported a family who lived in a
basement tenement where all six children helped make paper bags.
None of them, though American born, had been to school. There
was a small boy, his face flushed with chicken pox, sitting on a little
stool stitching knee pants. A little girl, in advanced stages of tuberculosis, was making cigarettes, "moistening the paper with her lips."
Disease was spread with the shipment of home-produced merchandise
from uninspected tenements to other communities.

Many social workers condemned parents for putting their children to work. A few immigrants believed women and children were
a man's private property and sources of his financial support, an
attitude common in their native countries. And in isolated cases,
fathers sat idly by while their sons and daughters scrounged for a

living. But Florence Kelley pointed out in an article that most children worked to supplement parents' inadequate wages, basing her report on an investigation of children in textile mills who worked ten to twelve hours a day, six days a week, breathing in poisoned dust. The public was aroused to these conditions by a strike in May, 1903, when 16,000 children under twelve years of age were among the 100,000 workers who walked out of the Philadelphia textile mills to demand a shorter work week. To dramatize the abuse of these striking children, the union organizer Mary Harris Jones, known as "Mother Jones," led a "March of the Mill Children" from the Pennsylvania mills to the summer home of President Theodore Roosevelt in Oyster Bay, Long Island. En route she addressed meetings, such as a rally of 1,500 on a New York City street corner, bringing to the platform factory cripples—little boys with fingers cut off and hands crushed by factory machines.

When President Roosevelt refused to see Mother Jones and her delegation of children, she was not mollified by the president's message that he sympathized with her efforts. She continued to inflame public opinion with her dramatic exposure of child labor abuses in factories, while at the same time books and magazine articles were exposing conditions of children who worked in canneries and the cotton fields. These actions strengthened the organized efforts of settlement house workers who would persevere in the fight against child labor. Mother Jones took the issues to the public; Lillian Wald and Jane Addams applied moral pressure through settlement houses and reform organizations; Florence Kelley through the National Consumers League. They pushed the state political machine into movement and in 1903 New York adopted its first substantial law establishing limitations on child labor. Still, in the absence of proper inspection, labor laws were ineffective and tenement sweatshops continued to flourish. Miss Wald also chaired a committee that worked toward keeping children out of hazardous street trades.

In 1904 Mrs. Kelley formed the National Child Labor Committee (NCLC), an outgrowth of a local organization she and Miss Wald and other settlement house workers had formed two years before. It brought into coalition social activists whose names would appear and reappear through the years in the general upsurge for reform: such people as Rabbi Stephen Wise of New York City's Free Synagogue; Oswald Garrison Villard, publisher of the liberal newspaper the *New York Post* and the magazine *The Nation*; Mary Simkhovitch, founder of Greenwich House; financier Paul M. Warburg; Dr. Felix Adler; Owen R. Lovejoy, General Secretary of NCLC; V. Everit Macy, businessman and philanthropist; Mrs. Emmons Blaine, a reformer and philanthropist. A meeting at Carnegie Hall called by NCLC in the spring of 1904 did not create much of a stir. Something bold had to be done, something to arouse people to urgent action.

At Miss Wald's breakfast table one morning in 1905, Florence Kelley, in her inimitable tone of outrage, was reading an item out loud from the morning's paper about the Secretary of Agriculture, who had been dispatched south to investigate a crisis threatening the U.S. cotton crop brought on by the boll weevil. This was a serious situation that commanded the attention of the federal government.

As Miss Wald saw it, it brought home to her "that nothing that could have happened to children would have called forth such official action on the part of the government." If a quarter-inch insect that could destroy a cotton crop was worthy of federal investigation, should not the conditions that destroy children be worthy of an equal effort?

Why not a federal bureau to care for the welfare of children, Miss Wald asked at the breakfast table. Why not? was Mrs. Kelley's enthusiastic response. Mrs. Kelley discussed it with Edward T. Devine, a Columbia University sociologist and head of the Charity Organization Society. Dr. Devine proposed it to President Roosevelt, crediting Lillian Wald with the idea. President Roosevelt would not see Mother Jones, but he would see Miss Wald, a friend from the days he visited at Henry Street. After discussions with Miss Wald and others, he supported a bill for a Federal Children's Bureau when it was introduced in the 1906 Congress.

That year Miss Wald sponsored another bill calling for the limitation of child labor in factories and mines. She devoted time and energy, working with the NCLC, to mobilize support for the Federal Children's Bureau and could report that many organizations and groups were now sponsoring the bill. In the coalition were 25,000 religious leaders speaking from their pulpits on "The Value of a Child." The bill was backed by national organizations of women's clubs, the consumers leagues, school alumni associations, and state labor committees. The letterhead of the National Child Labor Committee listed so many outstanding names as sponsors that joining in the outcry against child labor became fashionable. Newspaper publishers such as Adolph S. Ochs, environmentalist and professor of forestry at Yale Gifford Pinchot (later to be elected governor of Pennsylvania), and others added their voices to the clamor for protection of children, and the establishment of a children's bureau to be responsible for every aspect of a child's life. It was envisioned as a national research center, one that would suggest guidelines; inform the public about the birth rate, illegitimacy, congenital and preventable diseases; point out dangerous occupations, accidents, and crimes against children; and collect and classify information. "Ours is the only great nation which does not know how many children are born and how many die each year within its borders," said Miss Wald at one point.

Despite mounting public pressure, Congress would not open hearings on the bill. But President Roosevelt, reacting to the public outcry for progress and reform, felt the pressure and asked Miss Wald to arrange what became the historic first Conference on the Care of Dependent Children. It met in Washington in January, 1909.

Hearings on the bill for a Federal Children's Bureau brought Lillian Wald and Florence Kelley to Washington to make impassioned pleas on behalf of children. "If over $300,000 is being spent for the eradication of scabies in sheep and another $126,000 for the eradication of scabies in cattle, why not spend a small portion of these amounts to save one-fourth of our blind from being blind, to make the deaf to hear, and to give to those charged with the care of the wards of the nation [a] bureau of central information . . . ?"

The government maintained bureaus for animals, weather, navigation, statistics. Why not a bureau for children? Miss Wald asked.

"Are fisheries more important than children? Is not the examination of children as important as the examination of the geological structure and mineral resources of the National Domain? Is not the welfare of children of the Nation as important as 'gauging streams and determining water supply'? . . . For all these many purposes we are spending great sums of money," much, much more than the small sum being asked for a Children's Bureau.

At a dinner at the Willard Hotel that evening, Miss Wald was introduced as the "woman behind the bureau," and was seated next to Theodore Dreiser whom she knew, not as an author, but as the organizer of the National Child Rescue Campaign.

Frustrated and impatient at Congress's refusal to act on the bill, Miss Wald wrote to Jacob Schiff in December, 1910, asking him to send "a strong letter to the New York senators and congressmen that you know," because "it seems absurd that the bill for the Children's Bureau has not been brought to a vote."

At a Child Welfare Exhibit in Chicago that year, she spoke on her philosophy of child rearing. She claimed ignorance about new trends such as the recent studies in educational psychology and urged that children be treated not as statistics, but as individuals for whose needs one has human responses.

A year later, in May, 1911, she served on a committee of the second Conference on Charities and Corrections that successfully urged the government to aid dependent families in order to ensure a child's attendance at school regardless of family income.

And finally, in April, 1912, President Taft signed into law the bill that Lillian Wald and Florence Kelley had dreamed up and created seven years before. The Federal Children's Bureau was a reality. "I am bursting with happiness that the Government is now committed to formal responsibility for human welfare," she said.

Dedicated to the multiple functions of Henry Street, Miss Wald rejected the offer to become the first administrator of the bureau, and instead endorsed Julia Lathrop of Hull House as its chief.

In dreaming about what the bureau could accomplish, she visualized it as a "temple" to children, as a great center that would draw from all corners of the earth the latest information on child care, and educate teachers, parents, and health officials on the best methods available. In the bureau, she saw a "new conception of the child—free of motion, uplooking, the ward of the nation."

But Miss Wald's Children's Bureau did not bring an end to child labor. That struggle continued and thus she remained vigilant, attending meetings and speaking against industrialists, especially the owners of southern textile mills, whose exploitation of children was well documented.

"You are a pioneer as you know and must live up to the parade," Jane Addams wrote to Lillian Wald in January, 1915, about an NCLC meeting in New York. When Miss Wald was diverted to other pressing issues, Florence Kelley continued to lead the fight and finally won passage of a federal child labor amendment in 1924.

7

"Women No Longer Spin and Weave..."

L I L L I A N Wald was young, only twenty-eight, a gently nurtured woman from the flower city of Rochester, when she moved to Henry Street. In her two years at Jefferson Street, she had learned to feel at home in the Lower East Side. And encouraged by both Josephine Shaw Lowell and Jane Addams, she had become increasingly sensitive to the needs of the community. Creating playgrounds, recreation centers, and parks, and mobilizing coalitions against child labor were only strands of her social activism. For at Henry Street a settlement house was forming, evolving out of and flourishing alongside of the Visiting Nurse Service like a fresh new shoot springing from a strong plant.

Somehow, no matter how responsive she was to the goings on in the neighborhood, Lillian Wald found herself trailing behind. She never learned to speak Yiddish, for example, the language of 90 percent of the residents, making do with the German tongue with which she had grown up. But if she did not want to be completely isolated, an outsider, she had to learn the language of the trade union movement then taking root in every factory as workers tried to gain control over conditions in the workplace and in their lives.

At Jefferson Street, a neighbor had knocked at her door one evening to ask Miss Wald's help in organizing her shop. Miss Wald had been impressed by the spirit of the young woman, who after a long day's work went out evenings with books under her arm, obviously trying to improve her employment or—Miss Wald's guess—at least eager for soul-satisfying fulfillment. The young nurse was too busy to feel self-conscious about her ignorance. What was a trade union? To find out she went to the local library to read up on the subject. She discovered that the movement was young, formed into a national body a few years before, in 1888, with the founding of the American Federation of Labor, which had grown out of the Knights of Labor. Militant strikes had been led by craft unions, the first expression of organization among artisans.

The young woman outlined conditions in her shop, the sixty-hour work week, the unsafe working conditions. She had her worries, though, that membership in a trade union would seem "unladylike" and might even discourage marriage. She hoped that Miss Wald, an American born lady, would know how to handle such difficult matters.

When Miss Wald moved to Henry Street, another young woman, Minnie, who lived a block away, had asked for her help in a factory strike. Miss Wald gave the workers the use of the backyard for meetings and listened to their discussions, impressed by their eloquence. Miss Wald did not view strikes, or trade unions, as actions of the working class against the capitalist class. She still held the same simple belief that publicizing facts would bring change. When she arranged for a group of philanthropists to meet at Henry Street to discuss ways of helping "the working girl," Miss Wald invited Minnie to address them.

Minnie was blunt. "We are in the hands of the boss," she said. "What does he care for us? . . . We must work for bread now, but we must think of our future homes. What time has a working girl to make ready for this? . . . For all we know, soup grows on trees."

Miss Wald experienced the thrill of a trade union victory when Minnie invited her to celebrate a midnight contract signing in a "smoke-filled room in Walhalla Hall." Women were included in the contract, a rare concession, Miss Wald learned, for women found it difficult to get into the male-dominated unions.

The ramifications of the trade union movement became clear to her only as she joined her neighbors' struggles to make collective bargaining an effective weapon. All around her, like deeply engraved images, were the living conditions that working people endured, especially women, for whom she had special empathy. Low wages forced them to live "down to the bone," she said. They shared beds in tiny rooms, did their own cooking, cleaning, washing, and ironing of their shirtwaists. At work in poorly lighted, firetrap factories, they breathed contaminated air ten to twelve hours a day, six days a week. They paid for their own supplies of needles and thread, for locker space, and they paid fines for infractions of rules and petty charges they did not understand. Work, work, work, bent over machines making garments, artificial flowers, neckties, belts, boxes, "the whole long list of necessities and luxuries for other people," Miss Wald called it. Disease ended lives early, especially tuberculosis, the "White Plague" or "Tailors Disease." At an early age madness broke down the frail, or suicide brought a swift end to misery.

The streets were filled with women who became prostitutes, lured by pimps and procurers into thinking it an easier way to earn their keep. Such sights, implicit in violence and coercion, outraged Miss Wald's sense of respectability. "No stories of the red light district have told the tale, in my opinion. Buried deep in my soul are the pictures of what was the insult to womankind, the dragging down of mankind."

The conditions were familiar to Polish-born Morris Rosenfeld, called the "poet of the sweatshops." He worked in a factory to earn his bread and he read his poems of "the Sweatshop" at Henry Street gatherings and other meeting halls.

"So wild is the roar of the machines in the sweatshop,
I often forget I'm alive—in the din!

I'm drowned in the tide of the terrible tumult—
My ego is slain; I become a machine.
I work, and I work, without rhyme, without reason
produce, and produce, and produce without end.
For what? and for whom? I don't know, I don't wonder—
Since when can a whirling machine comprehend?"

The endless chronicle of ills was reduced to statistics. But statistics appalled Miss Wald. "Read each figure a human being," she begged. "Read in descriptions of sweatshops, factories and long working days the difficulty, the impossibility of well-ordered living."

In the struggle to organize shops, she saw not early failures, not tedium, nor dates and figures, but her neighbors, as heroic and stubborn as pioneers tilling rocky soil. The complexities of their situation could not fit a conventional canvas but required a mural or the triptych of medieval art. For women were oppressed not only as workers but because they were women, weighed down by a double burden. In the workplace they were paid lower wages than men, were victims of sexual harassment by foremen and bosses. Even worse, gender discrimination pervaded the trade union movement, and women were isolated from organizing efforts. Male-dominated unions claimed that women belonged in the home; they had marriage as their goal and were therefore only temporary workers, moving from job to job. With no lifelong commitment to an organization, women were considered deterrents to trade unions and above all, threats to male employment because they accepted lower wages for the same work. Women belonged at home!

A few of these claims were valid. Some employers were able to stay in business because they paid women and children low wages; women were unable to attend late-night meetings in shabby saloons. And like Minnie, many worried that they had no time to plan for marriage and home life. But tens of thousands of women were forced into factories to earn a living and they began to view the workplace as permanent. Improved working conditions were as vital to them as to their male counterparts. In their double oppression only employers gained. And the multiplicity of evils began to unravel only when women took matters into their own hands.

Miss Wald was kept informed of labor struggles by Leonora O'Reilly and her mother who became Henry Street "family" when they took a flat next door to the settlement. Miss Wald had met Miss O'Reilly in 1894 when they had both joined the Social Reform Club, and the young woman had impressed Miss Wald with her knowledge of factory conditions. She was hard working, articulate, and graced with dedication to her class. In a few years she was made vice-president of the club, for its bourgeois membership prized Miss O'Reilly, whose credentials were so impeccably working class.

She had been a factory employee from age eleven when she left school to take a job to supplement her widowed mother's paltry wages in a glove factory. At sixteen, she joined the Knights of Labor (where her mother was a member) and led her first strike. While at Henry Street, she organized a small group of women shirtmakers into Local 16 of the United Garment Workers Union. The parent body turned a cold shoulder to requests for financial and organizational support. Miss Wald helped her, provided meeting rooms, and wrote to the UGW leadership, urging them to open their ranks to women.

To give Miss O'Reilly the education she had never had and still wanted, friends subsidized her for a year. During that time she, Miss Wald, and a few other women set up a model garment workers cooperative in Henry Street where women learned fine sewing skills under optimum conditions. This too, like early efforts at trade union organizing, flared up and faded, another thrust at a slumbering colossus, the working class. But women's militancy was expressing itself in other ways.

In 1902 they poured out into the streets of the Lower East Side in a spontaneous mass boycott against butchers and the increased price of meat. Singled out by Jewish women were kosher butcher shops, which had not passed on price decreases to consumers. Over 5,000 women overflowed a protest meeting in Irving Hall, and in an unprecedented action, 500 police were called in to maintain order. They did so by pushing women around, beating a few with clubs, and hauling them off in paddy wagons. The unexpected brutality brought wider public support to the boycott.

"We will not permit retail butchers to give us bones and stones when we are paying for meat," said a speaker at a meeting. The Hebrew papers called it a revolution when the women, organized into the Ladies Anti-Beef Trust Association, took their boycott to Brooklyn, where again police cracked down, charging the women with looting. BROOKLYN MOB LOOTS BUTCHER SHOPS and RIOTERS LED BY WOMEN WRECK A DOZEN STORES, were the banner headlines in local newspapers. A *New York Times* editorial charged the women with being of a "dangerous class. They are very ignorant, they mostly speak a foreign language. They do not understand the duties or the rights of Americans . . .

"It will not do," the editorial continued, "to have a swarm of ignorant and infuriated women going about any part of this city with petroleum destroying goods and trying to set fires to the shops of those with whom they are angry . . ."

One woman boycotter, asked by a magistrate why she rioted, replied, "We don't riot. But if all we did was to weep at home, nobody would notice it; so we have to do something to help ourselves."

Lillian Wald believed in these women and in their strength. The education she received each day at the breakfast table from the "family" militants gave support to her instinctive sympathies and she took her place on the inside of labor's struggles.

Clearly immigrant working women needed help. The reluctant, sporadic cooperation extended by a union here and there left them unaffiliated. Into the void came middle-class social activists, settlement house workers, and leaders such as Lillian Wald and Jane Addams. These women were articulate, had energy, education, and skills, and were sincerely interested in rescuing the exploited and oppressed. So long as their affluence was not threatened, they worked side by side with their less fortunate sisters. In the process, many freed themselves from dull, routine lives. And they carried forward the legacy of women who had led the antislavery movement; women who were the backbone of charity work, of the Women's Christian Temperance Union, of the suffrage movement.

Miss Wald encouraged cross-class coalitions in both the settlement house and nursing services where community work was supported by upper-class people. Many of them, observing slum conditions firsthand, were roused to action.

But there were other forces at work in the crusade to organize workers, such as the Industrial Workers of the World (IWW), headed by "Big Bill" Haywood, building militant unions through radical tactics and talking about an international brotherhood. The Socialist party educated workers in Marxist principles of class conflict. Anarchists, single taxers and countless varieties of labor theoreticians addressed themselves to working-class problems. And there was a powerful contingent of social reformers, thousands of women and men pressuring the government to legislate change.

The isolation of working women in the early days of the trade union movement became a pressing topic of discussion among reformers. Among Miss Wald's friends was William English Walling, a wealthy Southerner who had already become an outspoken voice on behalf of trade unions, suffrage, and women's rights. He lived at University Settlement where he met Ernest Poole. Walling and Poole frequently came to lunch at Henry Street and joined Miss Wald, Mrs. Kelley, Miss Dock, and Miss O'Reilly in discussions about the labor situation. Encouraged by Miss Wald and her comrades at Henry Street, Walling went to England to learn firsthand how women there had organized an independent trade union movement. Back in the United States in November, 1903, he attended the annual convention of the American Federation of Labor at Faneuil Hall in Boston where he met with leading social reform activists and settlement house workers. Among them were Vida Scudder, Emily Greene Balch, professor of economics at Wellesley College, Jane Addams, Mary McDowell, a Hull House resident who had helped lead the Chicago stockyard strike, and Mary Kenney O'Sullivan, a Chicago trade union organizer who had moved to Boston. Out of discussions and meetings grew a bold idea. Fed up with the American Federation of Labor's isolation of women, and recognizing that in union there was power, they founded a unique body which they called the Women's Trade Union League (WTUL). Mary Morton Kehew, a public-spirited Boston aristocrat, became the League's first president; Jane Addams was elected first vice-president; Lillian Wald and Leonora O'Reilly were on the executive board. The first demands included equal pay for equal work, the eight-hour work day, and woman suffrage. The women, unaided by the men, would go it alone.

No explosion of fireworks greeted the formation of the WTUL. For years women looked for a glimmer at the end of a dark road. A group of dedicated volunteers staffed the organization and worked on immediate practical issues, organizing consumer boycotts and street meetings, supporting actions against rent-gouging landlords. They introduced businesslike procedures and handled publicity. When 125 women walked out of a paper box factory, WTUL women joined the picket line and raised bail money for those arrested.

While middle-class women were thus defining themselves as able leaders, they passed on their skills to the immigrant workers, whose legacy had been even greater passivity and subordination than their own. They encouraged them to assert themselves and to speak up at meetings. In the process, they also imbued the workers with their middle-class values and ideas of womanhood, not perceiving that different, distinctive class attitudes and concepts gave workers their own inner strength.

Miss Wald remained a dependable ally of trade union organization, a consistent source of support and encouragement. Occasionally she addressed trade union meetings. For a woman dependent upon upper-class financial backers to maintain her organizations, it was not always easy. Often she walked a narrow plank, forging her way between supporters and critics from the right and the left.

Radicals attacked settlement house workers for frequently allying themselves with conservative labor to oppose militant union tactics, and for shoring up society with piece-by-piece reform instead of seeking basic economic changes. Trade union organizer Gertrude Barnum claimed a settlement "introduced into [people's] lives books and flowers and music, and it gave them a place to meet and see their friends or leave their babies when they went to work but it did not raise their wages or shorten their hours."

Emma Goldman, gaining prestige as an anarchist, also leveled gibes at settlements. She often visited Henry Street to see her close friend, Emma Lee, employed in the Nurse Service. She conceded that Lillian Wald, Lavinia Dock and Helen McDowell were the first women she had met who felt an interest "in the economic conditions of the masses," as she put it; they had a genuine concern for the people of the Lower East Side. But, she wrote at a later date, "They come from wealthy homes," and though they had completely consecrated themselves to what they considered a great cause, their work was palliative. "Teaching the poor to eat with a fork is all very well but what good does it do if they have not the food? Let them first become masters of their life; they will then know how to eat and how to live."

On the other hand, conservatives who supported the Henry Street Settlement called Miss Wald a radical. They feared labor unions as intensely in the early days as a later generation would fear socialism and communism, as Miss Wald herself pointed out in *House on Henry Street*. She was no "Mother Jones," leading a crusade of working children, yet she brought to a standstill a dinner party for her financial supporters—bankers, industrialists, lawyers—when she mentioned in her address that she knew and respected a union delegate, "one of those heroic labor leaders, and it was a joy to me to have any part in helping him." Every knife and fork stopped in midair and her supporters accused her of "going over to the other side."

Her main financial backer, Jacob Schiff, was also squeamish about the extent to which Miss Wald was affiliating herself with the trade union movement. No one would deny her efforts on behalf of children—that was such a humane thing to do! But trade unions skirted class conflict and represented a threat. Nevertheless, when Miss Wald once described to Mr. Schiff the desperate conditions of families of strikers, he gave her and Miss Dock money to help out on the condition that the union know nothing about his contribution.

Miss Wald held to her course. She believed firmly in flowers, books, and music for workers. It did not put bread on the table. But flowers *and* bread, long before it became a fashionable slogan, reflected her conviction that workers should know life held more than work and sleep. Bright color, warmth, joy, love were among her weapons to help people fight poverty's paralysis, to arouse the mind against poverty's despair.

In a blistering article called "Organization Among Working Women," written in 1906, Miss Wald brought reality to the sentimental image of women who worked and made up 17 percent of the work force. "Women no longer spin and weave and card, no longer make the butter and cheese, scarcely sew and put up the preserves at home," she wrote. "They accomplish these same things in factories in open competition with men . . . and each other." Despite facts, she said, we "as a nation superstitiously hug the belief that our women are at home and our children at school." Far from it, she said. Women were in dangerous and unladylike jobs, swinging picks in mines, bending over looms in textile mills, eviscerating chickens in packinghouses. Men in government held on to an antiquated concept of feminine delicacy and thought women were still turning out "exquisite pieces of millinery and needlepoint." The time had come to accept the harsh truth.

Busy though she was in her efforts to get the Federal Children's Bureau established, and occupied with countless other responsibilities, she worked with reformers on the city, state, and federal levels in support of legislation to improve working conditions. She led a movement for state aid for the unemployed and convinced New York State Governor Charles Evans Hughes to appoint a commission to study the immigrant labor problem.

After years of sporadic activity, the women's trade union movement exploded into action when the shirtwaist makers went on strike in New York City in 1909. The strike would have vanished without a trace but hired thugs, protected by police, beat up and arrested a fifteen-year-old striker, Clara Lemlich, and other women pickets in front of the Leiserson Company and the Triangle Waist Company. The brutality brought a flood of workers to the tiny union headquarters in a Clinton Street tenement to join the union, Local 25 of the International Ladies Garment Workers Union (ILGWU).

Thousands turned up for a Cooper Union meeting in November, 1909, to discuss a general strike. The leadership vacillated when frail, but spirited Clara Lemlich spoke up. "I am a working girl," she said, "and one of those on strike against intolerable conditions. I have no further patience for talk . . . I move we go on a general strike in the trade!" A roar of applause greeted her words. Her message was speeded to overflowing meetings in nearby halls.

Twenty to thirty thousand shirtwaist makers went out on strike and made labor history. Seventy-five percent were women between the ages of sixteen and twenty-five, earning an average weekly wage of five dollars for a sixty- to seventy-hour work week.

For thirteen weeks of bitter struggle, women walked the picket line in cold and snow. Many were beaten up and arrested. The image of women as passive, submissive, and unconcerned with collective bargaining was smashed under their marching feet. At every step, WTUL women were at their side, staffing the office, raising bail money, picketing. Society women held rallies and raised money. Support eventually came from the United Hebrew Trades, the suffrage movement, the Socialist party, churches, students, and workers. But women were waging a complex battle, not only to arouse the public and male-dominated unions to their hideous conditions, but for their own growth. Working-class women developed into leaders. Clara Lemlich, already well known as a militant on the Lower East Side, became a public figure. So did Rose Schneiderman, a forceful orator who went on tour to raise money. She called wealthy women supporters the "Mink Brigade." To a church congregation she said, "You read editorials about cruelty to birds. Aren't these working women entitled to equal consideration with the birds?" Leonora O'Reilly, long an acknowledged leader, was in the forefront of the struggle. Pauline Newman, who started working at age eight and brought home $1.50 a week for a twelve-hour day, became a union organizer.

The strikers did not win union recognition but the national publicity given their cause won for them an irreversible sense of their own power and ability. Organized labor in the garment industry championed them and following their lead, undertook their own militant strikes.

Miss Wald's settlement was a center of support. She transmitted the strikers' needs to powerful and wealthy people whom she called on for contributions and bail money. Along with settlement house leader Mary Simkhovitch and muckraker journalist Ida Tarbell, she wrote letters to the press protesting police brutality. In her close identification with the neighborhood, nothing gave her greater pleasure than the courage shown by young immigrant women during the Revolt of the Twenty Thousand (or Thirty Thousand), as the shirt-waist makers strike of 1910 was called. She often spoke about them in her talks supporting unrestricted immigration. In a December, 1910, talk to a church group she told about a striker who turned down an extra five dollars a week to become a scab with the retort, "You cannot buy my conscience with money"; and about a working woman who had given up her nighttime study of dentistry to contribute her savings to her family while she was on strike. She would tell about Clara Lemlich, beaten up by thugs while she led pickets in singing Italian and Russian working-class songs. "Stand fast, girls," she shouted, though she had broken ribs and was being hauled off to jail.

Miss Wald explained to her audiences that immigrant working women were ready to suffer hunger, humiliation, brutality (in prisons) "for a cause they believed to be socially righteous." Two years after the strike she stated a straightforward position when she spoke on "Immigrant Women in New York" before the Brooklyn branch of the Consumers League. She supported the trade union movement, she said, as "the most immediate opportunity for self-expression and social service for the greatest number of working women," and "when the history of this period is written . . . it will be shown that the [women] who learned to stand together for higher opportunities and better shop and home conditions for all, have kept alive the most basic essentials upon which our Republican civilization stands."

Disputes, name calling, strikes, and in-fighting came to a climax when in March, 1911, a raging fire spread through the Triangle Waist Company on the tenth floor of a dilapidated building off New York City's Washington Square. One hundred forty-six women lost their lives, many by jumping out of the windows when they found the doors to stairways and fire escapes bolted. This custom enabled bosses to search employees for stolen goods at the end of the work day and also kept out union organizers. At a citizens meeting called by the WTUL at the Metropolitan Opera House a few weeks later, outraged women decried the needless tragedy. Miss Wald, in the audience, told an interviewer that no one could be insensitive to the speakers' anguish "over youth so ruthlessly destroyed." The fire focused public attention on sweatshop conditions and resulted in a rush of state legislation that years of effort by Miss Wald and others had not accomplished.

Trade union organization was booming and women had won their place but there were other schisms, revealed especially in the Women's Trade Union League. The 1912 Millworkers Strike in Lawrence, Massachusetts, brought conflicts to a head. The strike erupted suddenly when workers found a thirty-cents weekly cut in their pay envelopes. It meant five loaves of bread less for diets already dangerously close to the starvation level. Millworkers had a shorter life expectancy of thirty years compared to the average for professionals. Millworkers' children often did not make it to adulthood.

Strike leadership was in the hands of Bill Haywood, his coleader Elizabeth Gurley Flynn, and the Industrial Workers of the World. Rather than be identified with radical leaders like Haywood and Flynn, the Massachusetts branch of the WTUL and other moderate labor groups refused to support the strike. Thus they isolated themselves from the shameful working conditions and the just grievances of millworkers, the majority of whom were women and children. Again, as in New York City in 1909-1910, women emerged as militant leaders. "Better to starve fighting than to starve working," they shouted on the picket line. And because they dreamed they would one day lead full, decent lives, they added to their strike song, "Yes, it is bread we fight for—but we fight for roses, too!"

The winter was bitter and many families were without food. Police and militia were ruthless in their beatings and arrests of pickets. Striking parents, unable to feed or protect their children, agreed to a plan to send them to friendly communities offering shelter. Accompanying 119 children to New York City was nurse Margaret

Sanger, who had seen poverty in the Lower East Side during her years with Lillian Wald's Visiting Nurse Service. But never in all her nursing in the slums, she wrote in her autobiography, had she seen children in so ragged and deplorable a condition. "They were pale, skinny, shivering, emaciated. None wore woolen clothing; only four had overcoats—in a town that manufactured coats."

Lillian Wald found the Lawrence strike situation too grave to ignore and she went up to Lawrence to bring children back to the Lower East Side where families were waiting to house and feed them. Knowing how little most of these families had, she made sure there was adequate food. "I am so glad that you were able to go to Lawrence," wrote Jane Addams to Lillian Wald. "The actions of the police and militia there have sounded perfectly preposterous. I am quite sure that a [tsarist] Russian official would feel that we had gone him one better."

Miss Wald also arranged for a Lawrence striker to tell her story at a meeting at Henry Street. It brought an outpouring of support both in money and demands for justice for the strikers. But a few of Miss Wald's backers criticized her, saying she was using Henry Street for propaganda purposes. One or two withdrew funds for nurses' salaries.

She learned that whenever she took the progressive side in a controversial issue, funds from donors would dry up. It happened when her suffrage efforts became known, though she protested she was not a militant suffragist, and when she helped form a cloakmakers union. In her expanding work these were setbacks, for she needed every bit of financial support.

8

The Sun Shines
on Everyone

S H E had centered attention on the Lower East Side by helping the deprived demand a fair share of industrial society. Caught up in countless activities to make her neighbors visible, she did not fully perceive the scope of the first decade of the new century, which would be called the Progressive Era. Yet she was one of the leading figures in the great movement of people—labor, immigrants, women, children, blacks—toward greater social justice. The U.S. president during that epoch was her friend Theodore Roosevelt.

Fresh ideas spreading through the writings of scholars and journalists had buttressed these struggles. A collection of new facts declared laissez faire theories about individualism and the survival of the fittest obsolete. Anthropologist Franz Boas attacked racism; Thorstein Veblen criticized big business; liberal journalists and muckrakers Walter Lippmann, Ida Tarbell, Lincoln Steffens, and dozens of others exposed industry's corruption and greed. In Congress, liberal senators like Robert La Follette charged government with responsibility for public welfare. And locally, New York Mayor Seth Low called for the investigation of slum dwelling. In this changing landscape it had become a moral imperative to talk up against the overwhelming power of big business and government indifference.

At Henry Street Lillian Wald had become the focus for thousands. Youngsters as well as her peers looked to her for guidance, for inspiration, or simply for protection from undernourished lives. At first she was their voice. But she knew it was essential that people learn to speak up for themselves, that they become informed participants in the public debates.

The clubs founded at Henry Street opened the way for youngsters in particular to be educated, to "stretch out, for fun, fellowship, and responsibility," she said. They started in a modest way when a group of ten- to twelve-year-old boys asked to see her "when you are not busy." She arranged to meet with them Saturday night and that evening, in 1895, Henry Street's first club got under way. They called it the American Hero Club and Miss Wald herself became the leader, setting up a model for future clubs. She dramatized lives of men and women in history who had overcome obstacles to achieve success. Other clubs followed when someone with a special skill in dance, theater, cooking, carpentry, science, or current events offered to help community children.

Sometimes Miss Wald requested certain uptown people to become club leaders. They responded both to her moral convictions and to the spirit of the times. Those who ventured down to Henry Street to help out soon found themselves deeply involved in social activism.

One of those to visit Henry Street was Herbert H. Lehman, after his graduation from Williams College in 1899. He fell under Miss Wald's spell, seeing her as a "dynamic, energetic, indefatigable" woman "with vision." (Lavinia Dock struck him as "a peppery woman with great personal charm.") Mr. Lehman became head of the second boys' group, the Patriots Club, and led discussions and organized games and sports. Not a single youngster ever forgot the personable, responsive young man who went on to become governor of New York State and a U.S. senator. Nor did Mr. Lehman ever forget them.

Word spread among the youngsters about the goings on at Henry

Street. At Public School 147, Ely Siegel told Morris Golden that he had joined a Henry Street club. Morris, who lived only five doors down, at 255 Henry Street, joined the Patriots Club and began to spend all his spare time at the settlement. He took dancing lessons for three cents a week. He and his friends, playing on the street, would tip their caps to Miss Wald and Miss Dock when they saw the nurses "going around the neighborhood delivering babies free of charge."

Julius Harwood, who played the violin and liked sports, was drawn to Henry Street by its orchestra and gym. He ate his first olive at Miss Wald's table when she invited him and other sport-contest winners to dinner.

It was the nature of Henry Street to break new ground for youngsters, to show different models in leadership and life-styles. Julius admired the "lovely" Ysabella Waters, "a tall, fine looking woman" who played the piano and set an example, he thought, "to neighborhood roughnecks."

The camps at six dollars a week also stretched the vision of the youngsters. Ben Schoenfein took his first train ride up to Camp Henry at Mahopac Falls. He saw his first play when a club leader took his group to the Hippodrome to see Maude Adams in *Peter Pan*! To Ben, Miss Wald was a distant figure, somewhat like his school principal. She looked regal walking down the street, tall, straight-backed, a long necklace dangling down her dress.

For Hyman and Anne Schroeder and their family, Miss Wald was a savior. Their widowed mother of five had no way to support herself and her children. The two little girls of the family went to school on alternate days because they had to share one set of clothing. Only Miss Wald's concern for them, giving Mrs. Schroeder sewing to do and providing the family with health care, pulled them through their starving days.

Hyman Schroeder joined the American Hero Club and his sister Anne went to the Homemakers, typical of the traditional gender roles the clubs maintained. Boys learned history, carpentry, and machinery while girls studied sewing, cooking, and fashion design.

There was a Good Times Club for mothers, offering relief from their daily grind.

The Schroeder children made Henry Street their alternate home. At Henry Street Anne, who became a secretary, met a bright young man, Louis Abrons, who traveled from his home in the East 100s to join the Patriots Club. Herbert Lehman became Louis's personal hero and mentor, lending the young man $400 so that he could complete his education at the University of Michigan. And when Anne Schroeder married Louis Abrons, who had gone on to become a successful engineer, both Lillian Wald and Herbert Lehman were honored guests at the wedding.

Tucked away in countless autobiographies are comments, such as one by teacher and philosopher Morris R. Cohen, testifying to Miss Wald's pervasive influence. As a young man he was chronically ill. "During Christmas week I enjoyed a rest at Grandview through the kindness of Miss Lillian Wald, head worker of the Nurses Settlement on Henry Street. This helped me considerably . . ."

Within each she kindled hope as if she lighted tapers at an altar. She turned youngsters around, gave them guidance and leadership, and they would say she was crucial to their growth, and in many instances, to their emotional survival. Through her they saw an alternative to their bruised lives. Not only did she offer flowers and books but she taught them responsibility, one to the other and to the social order. And they fell in love with her. She was beautiful, flushed with energy, breaking into a broad, warm smile even as she taught and chided. She had time for everyone, for every child of the neighborhood. They became her "sons" and "daughters." Her correspondence proliferated when children grew to adulthood and kept her informed of their lives.

Arthur Sobel wanted Miss Wald to know, before he left for college in Colorado in August, 1902, that she was the only one during four years of a difficult and miserable life "who comforted me, and cheered me, and lifted me out of myself. Saturday was my red-letter day because to see you meant all the world to me." And when Miss Wald reproved him for not keeping in touch while at school, Sobel wrote, ". . . I plead guilty of . . . merely *not writing*. For I think of you every day. I never win a debate, I never learn a new fact, I never do anything which lifts me higher, but that I thank Heaven for it that it will some day help me to do that which will please Miss Wald. . . ."

Jacob Shufro wrote, "I feel conscious of the great debt I owe you personally. No one but myself can estimate how changed my life, my hope, and ambitions became when by chance the Cicero Club came under your influence . . ."

In the ferment of the Progressive Era a group of uptown women also found their way to Henry Street. They came from the wealthy Jewish crowd associated with the Schiffs and Loebs to do volunteer work in the Lady Bountiful tradition. Under Miss Wald's influence they developed into active reformers, financial supporters, traveling companions, and lifelong friends. Irene Lewisohn, Alice Lewisohn, Rita Wallach Morgenthau, and Nina Loeb Warburg added to the splendor of Henry Street's reputation by infusing the settlement with their talents and energy. They became club leaders and part of the educational program that brought new vision to club members. In the process of feeling useful and needed, they themselves changed. Not only did Henry Street provide conditions in which they could define their skills, but the Lady's love freed their emotions and liberated them from the customary restraints of upper-class propriety. They had found their own true voice and their letters to Lillian Wald are filled with affection and gratitude, as indeed are hers to them.

Leonard Lewisohn brought his daughter Alice to meet Miss Wald in 1904. The wealthy Mr. Lewisohn was a board member of corporations dealing in copper, silver, and coffee (among others) and had become one of Miss Wald's most generous supporters. In the manner of the day, he often asked the head resident to do small favors such as finding lodgings for six or seven young men at the Sheltering home who had been accepted into college. Along with his request he sent two tickets for the opera *Lohengrin*, urging Miss Wald and Miss McDowell to use them.

His daughter Alice, raised in a high-stooped Victorian brownstone on East Fifty-seventh Street, was fascinated by the jungle of color and movement on the Lower East Side. She found the settlement equally vital, a warm place, alive with a continuous flow of people. Her father spoke of Miss Wald as a genius and the young woman found the head resident a joy, "a lady of miracles."

After the early death of her mother and father, Alice Lewisohn turned to Henry Street and Miss Wald for comfort. In subsequent visits she took along her younger sister, Irene. The two were swept up in Miss Wald's embrace and into the work of the settlement. In Henry Street's classes and clubs, they found escape from their loneliness.

Talented and trained in dance and theater, they created festivals around Lower East Side traditions. At the end-of-year holidays, Henry Street was aglow with Christmas tree candles and Chanukah lights at the same time in the same room, a mingling, as Miss Alice (so the children addressed her) said, "of the spirit of the Jewish and Christian midwinter feast of light." They celebrated the Chinese New Year and Passover holidays with appropriate chants and rituals. To prepare the festivals, Miss Irene did research into old cultures and created choreography for dances, training members of the children's clubs as well as older people to perform, an experience that launched dancing careers for more than one child.

Their love for Miss Wald showed in generous gifts. Years later they would make Henry Street an avant-garde cultural center by building the quasi-independent Neighborhood Playhouse. The Lewisohn eighty-acre estate, Echo Hill Farm, became a Henry Street camp.

"Dear, dear loved Lady," Miss Alice would thus address Miss Wald. Miss Irene, after a trip to the Far East with Lillian Wald and Ysabella Waters, wrote, "Dear Lady Light . . . Why attempt to tell a clairvoyant all that is on one's mind? You know perhaps even better than I what the months of companionship with you and sister Waters have meant . . . I am making a special vow to be and to do. The world is so much more precious to me . . ."

Nina Loeb Warburg, daughter of Mrs. Loeb, who had perceived Miss Wald's abilities years before, was Jacob Schiff's sister-in-law, the wife of Schiff's business partner Paul Warburg. It was natural for her to join young women in club work at Henry Street. But she found in Miss Wald not only a head resident but a strong, attractive woman. From her country homes she wrote beseeching letters, urging Miss Wald to come for a visit. "If I did not fear that you would consider me the most selfish old wretch you ever knew, I would tell you, *how* disappointed I am that you are unable to come here next week! I just know that I, who have everything in the wide world have no right to feel that in addition to it all—I want you!" At another time, Mrs. Warburg wrote in urgency from Shrewsbury, New Jersey, telling Miss Wald that only a visit from her would help her through an illness. "Do whatever you like best [about traveling here], but come!"

Another young woman who would find Henry Street an answer to an empty life was Rita Wallach. Lovely looking, fourteen years younger than Miss Wald, and at loose ends after a decision not to enter college, she did club work in one of the many slots called "citizenship," "guidance," "crafts." Her administrative skills blossomed and in time she became the staff coordinator of all club activity. The children called her "Miss Wallop" but to Miss Wald she was "the Daughter."

"My dear, very dear," Miss Wald wrote when Miss Wallach was leaving for a summer vacation, "This is to say just once more that you have been much to me all winter and that I am grateful personally and for this loved Settlement that you are helping to build. It is built of people who care and love and you are one of the precious pillars—Come back to us in Fall but have a happy summer."

Miss Wald's love and warmth became a source of inspiration. "If it had not been for you," wrote Miss Wallach, "I should never had had my present conception of life and its possibilities and before us I see a long vista of mutually happy years . . . That is why one loves, it seems to me, so as to bring tenderness and beauty to all, and that has been your great lesson, beloved Mother of my spirit."

Miss Wald wrote back, "Beloved, America is a howling wilderness without you. I'd have to emigrate or something if you were not 'my chile'." And Miss Wallach responded, "Just once more I want to tell you how thoughts of you and feelings for you have gone deep into my life—everything that has stood for beauty has been inspired by you and the thankfulness I feel for my share of you, and the dear settlement can scarce be whispered . . ."

After Miss Wallach's marriage to Max Morgenthau in 1907, the two women continued their close relationship, Mrs. Morgenthau writing to Miss Wald in 1908, "Dearest . . . I shall never get over the wonder of it, all the beauty and sweetness that you have brought in my life, you and the dear Settlement family . . ." And a letter of no date tells Miss Wald, "you always have been and always will be my 'leading lady' and I have a feeling of deep gratitude and humility that the spark in me has been kindled by your flame . . ."

Not only was this group of devoted uptown young women an added resource to Henry Street, but another group made up of brilliant career women was attracted to the head resident herself. Mabel Hyde Kittredge, the boldest among them, took up residence at Henry Street at the turn of the century. The daughter of a prominent pastor of a Madison Avenue church, she was a curious blend of wit and arrogance, although she revealed her vulnerability to Miss Wald. Outstanding as a leader in the new field of domestic science, she and Miss Wald sparked organizations for social reform.

The inner circle called Miss Kittredge one of Miss Wald's "crushes" because she enjoyed Miss Wald's private company for a few years. But Miss Kittredge was in a bad temper when the Lady was too busy to see her. "And so the verdict has gone forth, I can't have you," she wrote from her New Jersey home at Monmouth Beach. "The big restless, but nevertheless restful ocean is rolling to our very door . . . Even you must want the ocean at times instead of Henry Street."

Her apology to Miss Wald was abject after she made a slighting remark about "your people." "I believe that I will never say again '*my* people and *your* people.' It may be that even though I have no prejudice, I have used words and expressions that have done something to keep the line drawn between the two peoples . . . I have learnt to love more in the last three years than ever before. I have realized that humanity is wonderful even when sin seems to crush it

. . . I will not again make a dividing line . . . I will say *our* people . . ."

Typically, Miss Kittredge felt the need to improve her work to win Miss Wald's admiration. "Your approval of my work is very dear to me, and it is easy with such a push to go on and do still better. I have felt very sure of your friendship this winter, and believe that you have in a way understood how hard I have fought for that balance and calm that is such a frightful lack in me, and was the reason for my break down . . . Come back [from your trip], get full to overflowing with rest and come back to us a leader [as you always are] and a friend and a power . . . Bless you dear. Come back to us soon, Lovingly," (and then the very formal) "Mabel H. Kittredge."

A Christmas letter to Miss Wald was bitter. "These may be 'merry' days but they starve one to death as far as any satisfaction in calm, every day loving and talking goes . . . I have a good deal to say to poor tired Lillian Wald . . . I suppose that I didn't really need your friendship as compared with some of the poor, starved, tired souls that you have given your helpful individuality to, supplementing their weakness with your . . . energy. I am not loveless nor lonely . . . What you have done for my career is nothing . . . whether I live my life honestly and am true to my best self is of some account, and it may be that I needed you in order to do this. I know it would be a loss out of my life if my thoughts of you, my love for you and my confidence in you were taken away . . ."

Frances Kellor belonged to this group of career women. A graduate of Cornell University and law school, she headed research into urban problems, and did a notable study on brothels and "the red light district," showing the spread of prostitution and venereal disease among the neighborhood's children. Miss Wald, to whom this aspect of life was searing, worked with Miss Kellor to reduce vice in the community. The flow of warmth between the two women smoothed their working relationship. ". . . of course I couldn't tell you, I never can, what an inspiration and help you are . . . But I do know that you are dear and beautiful and that I love you for it . . ." wrote Miss Kellor to Miss Wald.

Muckraking journalist Ida Tarbell also felt the healing quality of

Miss Wald's concern: "It was like you, dear Lady, to stop at midnight to write a comforting note to a tired woman . . . A good sleep has set me going cheerfully again and this dear note of yours gives me a sweet sense of the goodness of the world. With gratitude and love, Believe me your friend, Ida M. T."

These personal relationships no doubt fulfilled Miss Wald in significant ways, but if there was inner turmoil it was screened from view by the public face, and her "controlled manner," as others called it. Perhaps she accepted "crushes" as intrinsic to the inspiration that made women, men, boys and girls, pillars of her work. Her aura of strength enticed the emotionally homeless, as well as the strong, to whom she spoke a common language. Loving was her style, part of her nature, yet paradoxically, her love was not only a way of giving but a way of receiving. It bound people to her in eternal gratitude as if they could never do enough for the Lady.

But there were just so many hours in a day even for a woman of her vitality and she could not be accessible to all to whom her love appeared as a special message, a singling out—and who wanted to have more of the Lady's private time.

Though her inner circle tried to guard its sanctity, there was trouble brewing, as Lavinia Dock so wisely noted. Miss Dock chose to remain abroad for an additional year, in 1904, to which Miss Wald expressed disappointment. Miss Dock wrote to Miss Wald from Berlin, "Dearest Lady: I could not really imagine that you would feel badly over my stay . . . would have had to be more conceited than I am . . . You shine on every one with warmth like the sun, but it would be too vain to suppose that the sun was shining on one's own account, wouldn't it? Really I find myself getting so old and dull and ugly that I cannot imagine anyone feeling really one pang at getting me out of the way . . . Honestly I think I am pretty nearly too old to do good hard nursing . . . but I am sure too there is useful work for the older women to do also, of a rather different kind—I hope when I do get back I can find someplace on a shelf not too high up or far back!"

And another of the inner circle was finding it crowded at Henry Street. Ysabella Waters wrote to Miss Wald in the hectic years of the first decade of the new century, "I could have been away ¾ of the time this winter and you would not have known it . . . The atmosphere of the house is so tense, and it has been getting more tense all the time, and makes me cuss and irritable—so for the sake of the house and all the dear ones in it I feel that I must get away a few hours of the 24—I have not the least intention of giving up my work, and as for the settlement that has grown a part of me. I shall be here on tap just as much as I always have." But Miss Waters took her own apartment to be away from the tension in Henry Street. Harriet Knight, too, visiting her sick father in Philadelphia, Pennsylvania, in 1902, sounded a mournful note, "somebody is thinking about you a very great deal, and would be made very happy by just a few lines."

Her family in Rochester missed her. Letters from her nephews and niece (Julia's children), say, we "are awful lonesome for you."

In the busy schedule was a course she taught at Teachers College in clinical aspects of the profession. In those years Miss Wald and Miss Nutting, head of the Columbia University Department of Nursing, frequently exchanged letters, sometimes revealing the tensions between them. "Sister dear, take down your tomahawk," wrote Miss Wald to Miss Nutting. "It does not belong to me . . ." To which Miss Nutting promptly replied, "Dear Lady, I see your point and the tomahawk is down . . ."

The complex relationships became from time to time too much, even for Miss Wald. For the one most vital to her work, her mentor and supporter, Jacob Schiff, also wanted more of her time.

Florence Kelley, about 1900

Jane Addams

Henry Street children

Henry Street playground

Children aged 5 to 12 making artificial flowers. Mother holds one-year-old child in her arms

Coming Home from Fresh Air Vacation (Battle with the Slums). Two little Mott Street girls

Strike leader Clara Lemlich

Leonora O'Reilly and her mother

Striking shirtwaist-makers selling copies of the *Call*, 1909-1910

The Civic Club

Tenth anniversary of the American Hero Club, October 1905. Seated: Lillian D. Wald. Standing, second and third from left: Aaron Rabinowitz, Helen McDowell. Standing, right and second from right: Harry Z. Cohen, Hyman Schroeder

On vacation: Lillian Wald and Ysabella
Waters (both seated), with Jane
Hitchcock

Lillian Wald, Mary Roget Smith and
unidentified child at Bar Harbor,
Maine

9

The Lady and the Philanthropist

I N the surge of events all the world was finding its way to her door—the sick, the healthy, the famous, and the needy. She added new programs like gifts of the gods, a scholarship fund to keep talented poor children in schools, vocational guidance classes to upgrade workers skills, debating and literary societies, a gymnasium, a savings bank, clubs, theater and dancing classes. Her advice was sought by nursing organizations around the world, by social reformers, and politicians.

At her table she entertained author John Galsworthy, anarchist theoretician Prince Piotr Kropotkin, and the 1905 revolutionary Katherine Breshkovsky (known as Babuschka); foreign dignitaries Ramsay and Mrs. MacDonald, Beatrice and Sidney Webb; Rabindranath Tagore, the poet of India; borough presidents, mayors, and governors. Never ending was the line of delegations asking her help —against the extension of an elevated loop, for better garbage removal, for police protection, or requests to serve on new committees. She was linked to every organization concerned with social welfare, including the little-known "Association of Practical Housekeeping Centers," headed by Mabel Hyde Kittredge, and the mayor's Pushcart Commission to license vendors.

She was unable to put a stop to the expansion of her activities. "I hear so much about you wherever I go, and am glad to find you taking your place alongside of Jane Addams in the popular consciousness, that's where you belong," wrote Jacob A. Riis to Miss Wald in a 1904 letter.

The empire she represented was vulnerable and she knew it, for the larger it grew the more money she needed. About half her income came from fees paid to nurses. There were also dribbles of funds sent in by the needy themselves. "I see in the papers," wrote one woman, "that you need money. You took care of my little boy when he was so bad burned and all my life since then I pray God, make me rich so I can help you big. But he hasn't answered my prayer so I send you this which I know isn't much but it is all I have." Enclosed was a ten-dollar bill. The generous poor, however, could not subsidize her work. Funding came from her "friend of friends," as she called Jacob Schiff, and from many in the German-Jewish community. It is questionable whether Henry Street would have been able to function in the early years without Schiff's support.

He and his mother-in-law had started Lillian Wald off with pin money. But by 1910 Miss Wald required tens of thousands of dollars for her budget. Henry Street was only one of Mr. Schiff's many philanthropies, for though he was a financial tycoon schooled in competition and involved in interlocking directorates with Morgan and Rockefeller banking, and railroad and steel combines, nevertheless, he kept his finger on the pulse of Jewish affairs.

In addition to being a brilliant financier, he was also a stable family man, urbane, politically and socially conservative. He shaped Jewish philanthropy by contributing 10 percent of his income to charities and humanistic causes and urging members of the German-Jewish community to do the same. Among organizations he subsidized were the United Jewish Charities, the Hebrew Infant Asylum, Montefiore Hospital, the Educational Alliance, and later on, the American Jewish Committee. He also endowed buildings for Harvard and the Jewish Theological Seminary as well as a social hall for Barnard College. Well deserved was his reputation as the most generous philanthropist of his time in an era when public welfare depended solely on private support. It was a mark of Lillian Wald's great aptitude in personal and public relations that she became Mr. Schiff's close friend and could command his attention for every detail of her work. By the turn of the century she sent him year-end instead of monthly reports and they were continuously in touch by phone, letter, and shared meals at either his Fifth Avenue home or the Settlement. Affection for each other suffused their relationship. In a 1905 New Year's Day exchange of vows of friendship he returned her warm wishes, "If we are beloved by you so are you by us and if as you say, our friendship . . . does mean something to you, so have we become more imbued with the spirit of responsibility wealth should impose upon those to whom it is given by Providence . . ."

Miss Wald personalized his giving, brought before him the names and faces of needy people. She met with him, not in an executive suite, but at Henry Street where he and his wife often dined. He traveled down to see her, through the poverty-stricken streets, a visible reminder of conditions he deplored. And the "family" figured in his affection for Henry Street. Frequently he asked that Miss Waters or Miss McDowell join Miss Wald for lunch at his residence. At his summer home in Maine, he entertained other friends of Miss Wald's, Jane Addams and Mary Roget Smith, who had a summer cottage nearby. The time came when Miss Wald's acclaim as a public figure enhanced his image as a liberal benefactor.

Having launched Miss Wald's work in 1893, Jacob Schiff continued to feel responsible for what went on at Henry Street. He was increasingly generous, making large and small contributions to meet the schedule of programs. In addition to a basic commitment, he gave her $100,000 in 1901 for the East Side Social Halls Association which built Clinton Hall, a community center of club rooms, restaurant, and a ballroom to replace the shoddy saloons generally used for social gatherings. He contributed regularly to her emergency fund, gave her money to electrify Henry Street, to build an icehouse in Nyack, New York, and to pay her secretary's salary. His firm, Kuhn, Loeb and Company, advised her about investments for

Henry Street funds, and eased her way when Mr. Schiff was out of the city. In the early days, Schiff tutored Miss Wald about the niceties of approaching the wealthy for contributions, to remember their birthdays and anniversaries, to "style her requests to fit the moods and persuasions of her potential supporters." Through him she gained access to the German-Jewish community, to the Felix Warburgs, the Paul Warburgs, the Lewisohns, the Lehmans, the Morgenthaus. Through other support circles she had behind her the Harknesses, Blaines, Belmonts, and McCormicks.

No matter how much money she raised, it was never enough and she became preoccupied with raising funds, putting her charm and wit to use on potential contributors. Those who knew Miss Wald as a brilliant conversationalist and asked to sit next to her at a dinner were advised by Mr. Schiff to "deposit a check with [him] for a thousand dollars for the Henry Street Settlement."

She broadcast her need to friends and acquaintances. "I am sorry you have to bother about money," Lavinia Dock wrote from Europe. "Surely all those men and directors will not leave you in the lurch with the worry of making ends meet?"

Her dependence on Jacob Schiff created difficulties. Frequently her artlessness masked maneuvering, for though they shared a common goal to improve conditions on the Lower East Side, they had philosophic differences. Jacob Schiff saw her as an intermediary for his philanthropy, and therefore tried to fashion her thinking to comply with his conservative point of view; but Miss Wald won her points when it involved her integrity.

Jacob Schiff's wealth derived from capitalist society and he zealously guarded the status quo, opposing actions that would threaten the economic structure. Still, he was not without heart, and he supported programs alien to his experience or interests such as Miss Wald's fight against child labor. On the other hand, he was cautious about the exploding trade union movement though he agreed with Miss Wald that degrading factory conditions should be improved. Rather than mass action, he preferred personal persuasion, and what he called "a just and orderly manner of change." He put pressure on employers, especially in the garment industry, to make concessions.

He did so to strengthen the economic system as well as to express sympathy for a wretchedly exploited working class. As Miss Wald knew, he responded to her descriptions of poverty-stricken workers, especially during a strike, and more than once, gave her money so that Henry Street could give urgent relief to strikers' families. However, the arbitration room was his chosen medium whereas Miss Wald also accepted the labor strike as an essential weapon.

They both agreed that immigrants should be assimilated into American society. For Mr. Schiff, the sooner this was done the happier he was, for as in Rochester and other urban centers, the German-Jewish community did not welcome the immigrants with open arms. To Americanize the newcomers, Miss Wald set up classes at Henry Street in language, citizenship, hygiene, and vocational guidance. They were taught how to speak up, how to express themselves as responsible members of a democracy, and above all to learn "to judge what was good in American life." The immigrants were also orientated toward American values—individualism, achievement, and success.

Immigrant leaders resisted this crash course in Americanism, this rush to fit newcomers into the American mold. While immigrants were still herded together in crowded tenements, their ethnic customs and identities were washed away, leaving them rootless—neither European nor American. And, immigrant leaders asked, Whose version of Americanism were the immigrants to suit? Which set of judges—Mr. Schiff, Miss Wald—the socialist, the anarchist, the Lady Bountiful?

Miss Wald respected her neighbors' ethnic pride and she encouraged festivals to celebrate their holidays, displaying their native songs and costumes on proper occasions. In a way she made museum pieces of their folkways. For she agreed with Mr. Schiff that assimilation was essential in order to absorb the immigrant into the mainstream and open doors to future success. It would also calm the growing clamor to restrict immigration. A new body of articulate opinion was pressuring government to close off the inflow of foreigners who were clogging the marketplace and putting native workers at a disadvantage.

At the same time that Miss Wald urged immigrants to upgrade themselves, she stressed the point to others that they were brought here in the first place as a cheap labor force for expanding industry. In a newspaper interview, she blasted the government for irresponsibility toward immigrants, for wasting human resources:

> Our waste of human beings on the great east side of New York is infinitely greater than our waste of natural resources in the whole domain.
>
> It is my belief that we in the United States have been doing exactly that which we pretend not to do, what we have solemnly declared we never shall do. We have denied the many very worthy human beings that dignity which should be accorded to every human being . . . We are dragging down, not building up . . .
>
> We promise opportunity to all, but do not keep our promise. If newcomers really have opportunity they usually get it only after fighting for it . . .

On the question of religion, especially as it affected immigrants, Miss Wald and Mr. Schiff had a basic disagreement. She had built a secular settlement house, as she explained in a letter to the editor of a book who asked for an interview. ". . . all my work has been nonsectarian and my interests are entirely nonsectarian. I am, therefore, not sure that I properly belong in your book since the title suggests work done by women as Jews." She elucidated her position further to the head of a Protestant college in Beirut, Syria, in answer to a query: "the Settlement is not connected with any institutional church . . . [Among us] are Protestants, Catholics, Jews, Colored people, and Japanese . . . people of all races and all creeds . . . believing in values of tolerance, kindness, and love." She herself had joined the Ethical Culture Society, dedicated to the value of good deeds and not religious faith.

While Miss Wald was attending nonsectarian services, Jacob Schiff was worshiping at Temple Emanu-El, a Reform synagogue where he was a devoted member. Though he wanted Jewish immigrants to assimilate quickly, he did not want them to lose their Jewish identity. He kept his eye on every effort that weakened religious faith, and in 1903 he enlisted Miss Wald's help in a delicate situation. It came to his attention that Jewish children at the Jacob A. Riis Houses attended a program addressed by an evangelical speaker, and were thus exposed to the Christian gospel. As a result of Miss Wald's discussion with Mr. Riis, it was agreed that Jewish children could attend these lectures only with the written permission of their parents.

Schiff also took exception to Christmas decorations at Henry Street, seeing them as "tempting" Jewish children from their faith at an impressionable age. Using himself as a model for assimilation, immigrants were to be Americanized in language, habits, and cultural attitudes but hold fast to their religion. For Miss Wald, Christmas decorations reflected her view of the settlement house as a place for social and religious integration on every level.

After his criticism, Miss Wald eliminated Christmas decorations from Henry Street. The swiftness of her act shocked Mr. Schiff. He hastened to explain that he had an aversion to the Christmas tree in "purely Jewish juvenile gatherings," that "nothing is further from me than the wish to deprive your gentile co-workers from the pleasure of a festival which is peculiarly their own, and as far as I am concerned, I would beg you, not to suppress in the future any Christmas Gala . . . so long as such is intended for those who have the right to it."

Other differences between the two emerged over the years. In 1903 Miss Wald proposed that Henry Street become legally incorporated.

How big do you want the settlement to become, Schiff cautioned. Young ladies attracted to it because "it is a family will find it less so if it becomes an institution like other organizations," he wrote.

Nevertheless, he would be satisfied with whatever conclusion she reached and Henry Street became an incorporated entity in 1904. Serving on the first board of directors was Jacob Schiff, along with Miss Wald, John Crosby, Lavinia Dock, head nurse Jane Hitchcock, Ysabella Waters, V. Everit Macy, and a few others. To help raise money to pay nurses regular salaries, Miss Wald established a fund-raising arm for the settlement, the "Visiting Nurses Permanent Fund," which began to absorb more of her time than all her other work. For Schiff was right, the larger she became the more money she needed, and she tried to broaden the financial base. By 1906, she had to find financing for twenty-seven nurses, the largest staff of nurses engaged in a single district in the United States.

On another issue Schiff won the day. In 1906, the English psychologist and political scientist Graham Wallas became the first male resident of Henry Street. Others soon followed and this development brought from Mr. Schiff a lengthy letter marked "personal." He again raised the question of the settlement becoming unwieldy, tracing its modest beginnings as district nursing into "all kinds of neighborhood work," and many new members coming into the family. But "you," he wrote to Miss Wald "not only remained the center, but also the directing spirit, to whom all look for guidance and advice. Thus your responsibilities have grown year by year and the entire structure of the settlement with its branches and workers exist because of your wonderful capacity for leadership, because of your exceptional personality, but the *larger* the settlement grows the less likelihood there is, that it will continue to exist after you." He advised her to draw a line somewhere, in the event that she and "some of the good ladies at your side, are taken out of it." Then he came to the crux of his letter, the question of male residents. "I am entirely frank to say, it has not my approval. I cannot bring myself to believe that even with the best and highest motives, the example of men and women living under the same roof, without ties of family life, can have a healthy effect upon those over whom you and your associates exert so large an influence and who will be certain to conclude without understanding the situation . . . that what is right for you, must also be right for them . . . I must risk telling you this; you know how deeply I am interested in you and your work, and I assure you, you have been more in mind these last eight days, than at any time since we know each other."

She acceded to his wish that she remain within "proper" bounds of society but a few years later, records show that Howard Bradstreet and Dr. Henry Moscowitz became residents at Henry Street. Among other male residents were Leo Arnstein, who would become secretary of the borough of Manhattan, and Bruno Lasker, a German intellectual, who lodged at Henry Street in return for club work and other assistance.

Mr. Schiff frequently rejected outright some of her suggestions. He thought her wish exaggerated to go with Ysabella Waters to Russia after the 1905 Revolution to offer nursing services to the anti-Tsarist forces. "Such a self-sacrificing offer was not needed," he advised her. And when at the end of 1905, she suggested that she mortgage the Henry Street property to raise money, Schiff replied in emphatic terms that his partner Paul Warburg and he "are both very clear . . . that you would have no right to mortgage the property of the settlement . . . , and indeed I would like to have your assurance that nothing of this sort will be done, now or in the future."

To her statement that she would like to do something for "colored people" (as black people were then called), he was enthusiastic. By all means do so, he said, "One God made us all." Mr. Schiff consistently expressed support for every effort of Miss Wald's to integrate the nursing service and attended Henry Street receptions for distinguished black leaders such as W. E. B. Du Bois.

In the 1906 election both Miss Wald and Mr. Schiff supported Republican candidate Charles E. Hughes for governor of New York State against newspaper publisher William Randolph Hearst running on the Democratic ticket. Miss Wald never commented on the irony of the situation, that her endorsement was significant even though she herself could not go to the polls to vote! A year after his election, Governor Hughes appointed Miss Wald and her colleague Frances A. Kellor members of "A Commission to Inquire into the Condition, Welfare and Industrial Opportunities of the Alien in the State of New York." Miss Wald had taken a decisive stand for unrestricted immigration and spoke at club meetings and civic auditoriums about the contributions of immigrants to the United States.

She loosened her tight grip on her responsibilities when an emergency call notified her that her mother had been hit by a trolley car and had been rushed to the hospital. Anguished, she fled to Rochester to find her mother resting comfortably. But her brother-in-law, Charles Barry, of whom she was very fond, had been critically ill, and died a few days after her arrival. She stayed on for several weeks, comforting her sister, Julia, and getting to know Julia's three children, Harriet, Tom, and Alfred. While in Rochester, she was in continuous communication with Mr. Schiff, who wrote cheerful letters sending warm greetings to her family, especially to her mother whom he had met at Henry Street a few years before. Others wrote, among them Florence Kelley. "It was an anxious story which Miss Waters told of your family! Do give my love and sympathy to Mrs. Barry! And keep for yourself all you can use thereof. It is a poor useless thing, but abundant!"

Back in New York, she resumed her countless responsibilities, greeting Governor Hughes as a dinner guest at Henry Street, testifying in Washington in 1908 on behalf of the Children's Bureau, which Schiff made every effort to attend so that he could hear her testimony. There were moments for pleasure such as Mr. Schiff's invitation that she dine with him and Mrs. Schiff and go on to see Isadora Duncan "in her classical dancing." ". . . perhaps this would interest you, too," he wrote.

During the ten years in which Miss Wald was growing into a leading public figure, she launched projects that would alter the nature of health care in the entire country. She thought of public health nurses as missionaries, penetrating rural as well as urban areas, bringing health education and medical attention to isolated and abandoned people. This vision stemmed from her conviction that health care was a basic right. With that belief in mind, she formulated a plan for a rural nursing service. She made the suggestion at the home of New York mayor George B. McClellan in 1908, and followed it up with letters stating that nursing care should be extended "to scattered dwellers in rural regions," such as had been developed in Great Britain and Canada. "In a country dedicated to peace it would be fitting for the American Red Cross to consecrate its efforts to the upbuilding of life and the prevention of disaster, rather than to emphasize its identification with the ravages of war," she said, thus directing the American Red Cross into peacetime activities. She persuaded Jacob Schiff to launch rural nursing with an initial grant of $100,000, which established for the Red Cross a

Department of Town and Country Nursing. Stories reached head-quarters in later years of nurses fording streams, riding horseback, and wearing snowshoes in isolated areas, to bring to long-neglected rural families the skill and care of the public health nurse.

That same year, 1908, Miss Wald convinced the Metropolitan Life Insurance Company to set up a nursing program for industrial policy holders, using Henry Street nurses. The success of the pilot project led to nursing care for policy holders in 1,200 other cities and the institution of similar services by other insurance companies.

Where would all the nurses come from? was her next concern. Not enough women (for this was exclusively a woman's career) were being trained for the jobs. What was needed was a corps of teachers to train nurses. To implement this need, Miss Wald convinced Mrs. Helen Hartley Jenkins, looking for a worthy philanthropic cause, to bequeath a large sum of money to endow Teachers College of Columbia University with a postgraduate school for teacher nurses. The program, administered by professor of nursing Adelaide Nutting, trained thousands of nurses who then spread out into rural and urban areas.

Exuberant about the growth of nursing, she saw "the whole movement . . . full of promise for homes, schools, and communities." Nurses were checking on epidemic disease, milk inspection, infant health. She made Henry Street the fulcrum for these programs, tying academic studies at Teachers College to practical experience at the settlement. She also lectured at the school, and advised foreign students from all corners of the world on how to build a public health service in their countries.

The promotion of all these areas of nursing ran parallel to her work on behalf of children, trade unions, clubs, woman suffrage, and every other cause concerned with progress.

The year 1909 opened with the usual greetings from hundreds of well-wishers. Florence Kelley wrote, "I have made a New Year's resolution . . . I am starting at noon today to be nice, and say only agreeable things, especially about the absent . . . This is due to the force of your example."

That year Carrie Chapman Catt, head of the National Woman

Suffrage Association, asked Lillian Wald to run for the state legis-
lature. "The politicians need a shock . . . So we offer you a possible
great honor and the risk of defeat, of course. We want you to consent very, very much . . . Hoping you will offer yourself a willing
victim upon the altar of New York womankind."

Miss Wald had not made woman suffrage her top priority, but
had been emphasizing the important fact that woman suffrage, to
gain a victory, had to win over not only the middle class but also
immigrant, working-class women, an idea supported by Jane Addams. She declined Miss Catt's offer, writing in reply that she could
not relinquish the "deep moral responsibility . . . from grave duties
that no one else could assume!" Loyalty to colleagues and consideration for "the people who place means in my hands ensures the
gravest devotion to them and our interests."

By 1909 even Jacob Schiff had to acknowledge that Lillian Wald
had achieved a level of success and public acclaim that called for
less monitoring of her activities by him. "Indeed," he wrote, "there is
no necessity for sending me on New Year an account of your activities during the year. You and the ladies associated with you are
constant living accounts of your great value, not only to the community, but to mankind in general and my only wish to you is that
you may remain long undiminished in health and strength, but also
that because you are so much needed, that you do not give too much
of yourself, which I am afraid you do from time to time." Repeat-
edly he advised Miss Wald, "You must husband your strength . . . or
sometime this continual living on your nerves will revenge itself, and
we need you." Mr. Schiff had become convinced that Henry Street
"will have its moments in history."

But there were meetings of new organizations to attend to as well
as the ongoing heavy schedule. Along with W. E. B. Du Bois,
William English Walling, Jane Addams, and other leading liberals,
she signed a call to a conference in 1909 to take action against the
violent outbreaks of racism in the country. On the eve of the conference, out of which grew the National Association for the Advancement of Colored People (NAACP), Miss Wald gave an

informal reception at Henry Street, and she remained one of the "Association's first and oldest friends."

Her vacations too were mixed with work. Only when she escaped to the Caribbean islands of Jamaica or Cuba, or to the Maine seashore or to Rochester to be with family, did she briefly free herself from mounting responsibilities.

In 1910, she planned a vacation to Japan with members of her inner circle—Ysabella Waters, Harriet Knight and Irene Lewisohn —only to find Jacob Schiff hovering over her, arranging for business acquaintances in Japan to meet her, to assist, and entertain her. He advised her what to do in Yokohama, what hotels to stay at in Kosho and Nagasaki, and where to eat in Tokyo. In his parting note to Miss Wald, he wrote, "It is customary everywhere that salaries are continued during vacations, and this should be so in your case . . ."

Armed with Mr. Schiff's letters, she got a behind-the-scenes look at the way Japanese millionaires lived. On her own she investigated the ongoing struggles for liberation from feudal slavery, the condition of the populace at large. While she, Miss Waters, and Miss Knight were examining the health situation and nursing care, Irene Lewisohn was researching the religious dramas of Japan called *Nōh*, which grew out of ancient temple dances. Miss Lewisohn later introduced this exotic style of dance into the Henry Street settlement through the Neighborhood Playhouse, which she and her sister Alice founded.

Seasickness while crossing the Pacific Ocean had made Miss Waters deathly ill and she refused to return the same way. The group changed its itinerary and traveled westward, making China the next stop. The poverty in China did not shock Miss Wald so much as the arrogance and cruelty of the Western occupation forces. In angry letters home, she asked—How could the world improve, if human beings are innately cruel?

By way of the Trans-Siberian Railroad, the travelers cut across the Russian steppes to spend a few days in Moscow. Disappointed at not being able to locate Madame Breshkovsky, the Russian revolutionary who had visited Henry Street a few years before, they continued on to western Europe, and sailed home across the Atlantic, reaching New York six months after their departure. Miss Wald was euphoric at being back on the Lower East Side, to be with her people, to feel enveloped once again in the love of neighbors and friends.

Mr. Schiff, who missed the "soul" of the family, informed her after a visit to his home, "It was such a delight to see your dear face once more and . . . the taste was good enough but only as a sample, and we want more of it as soon as you can conveniently come again . . ."

Her mounting burden of work alarmed her friends and they tried to make her life easier. But she had her own style, writing to Rita Wallach Morgenthau from Bethel, Maine, at the end of December, 1910, "Dearest: No!—you must not let anybody get the settlement an automobile . . . When I am decrepit and really unable to jump on or off the [trolley] cars, we can talk about it."

Did she have doubts? Was she ever worried that she was fighting the same struggles over and over, that perhaps she had not chosen the right direction? Or was she the way Mabel Hyde Kittredge saw her: "it wasn't what you did. It was your wonderful ability to separate clearly, distinctly, courageously the one right course, the one unerring moral instinct from the midst of all other considerations . . . It's what you are in your wonderfully sweet way to the people—it seems to me sometimes that your voice has the sweetest sympathy in the world in it."

But then came a letter from Ysabella Waters, who was vacationing in France in August, 1911, raising basic questions: "the rich are dreadfully ignorant," she wrote, "and we do not help them in the least when they dine with us. A plain but good dinner, much mahogany, large airy rooms nicely furnished—what can all these things tell of the awful needs of our neighbors—of their unlivable homes, their scanty meals, their long hard working days. Much could be done if the rich were not unfeeling as well as ignorant . . . When I had finished 20 years at Henry Street, I felt terribly depressed—so many years spent, so much thought and energy—and only a drop in the ocean has been changed— . . . all the settlements seem palliative

—they do not strike to the heart of the trouble—can they ever be anything else?"

Nor did Miss Wald express the kind of doubts about which Jane Addams wrote. Miss Addams said that she knew she was able to flee from the slums of Chicago to the Maine woods because her wealth rested on the labor of workers; that they generated profits for the leisure life of the upper class.

Miss Wald was not by nature or training philosophic. Nor did she use popular theories of class conflict and exploitation as tools to interpret society. She remained pragmatic and immediate in her approach to problems and derived satisfaction from being able to point to solid achievements. Perhaps they did not bring about basic economic change and permanent solutions, but she helped bring about the decline in infant mortality, the decrease in communicable disease, the phasing out of tenement labor, and the needy cared for in their homes when ill. She moved swiftly to resolve problems that interfered with her work, so that her energy could be productively used. Such was her experience on the Joint Board of Sanitary Control which had been appointed to establish health standards in the garment industry.

She and her colleague Henry Moscowitz learned that they could control sanitary conditions better in closed or union shops. Thus she supported trade union organization in the industry only to be rebuked by Jacob Schiff who complained that the efforts made "by you and Dr. Henry Moscowitz to create prejudice against employers" were unacceptable. Some time later he reminded her that social workers should not become overbearing but should stick to their particular work. These remarks prompted her to resign from the Joint Board of Sanitary Control.

At about the same time she also resigned from the Women's Trade Union League, an act that no doubt reflected policy differences with the national organization about the Lawrence, Massachusetts, millworkers strike as well as her loss of financial contributors for supporting the strike.

But Jacob Schiff's anger had a way of dissolving into unexpected tenderness. After he expressed annoyance at her trade union work, he wrote, "But with all you know, how dear and near you are to me and that I would do aught to make you happy and permit naught to come between us."

She was suffering from the exhaustion of heading expanding organizations. Despite everyone's advice that she take care of herself, she continued to work at top speed. On a trip to Chicago in 1912, she became ill and was forced from her desk and the public eye by a serious attack of pleurisy. She spent weeks at Lake Placid, in upper New York State, recuperating. Many letters of deep affection and concern were forwarded to her confirming her importance to the reform movement. "Dear Lady of the Generous Heart . . . Be good for our sake and take care of yourself," wrote Mary E. Dreier, director of the WTUL. And Florence Kelley penned a note to "Beloved Lady," signing her warm wishes with "Your loving old F. Kelley." Henry Moscowitz wrote, "I hope you will stay away until you are completely well . . . you are too precious to your friends and to the country, to be combatting nature at the same time that you are fighting the battles of social righteousness."

The summer of 1912 saw the gathering of new political forces for the presidential election. The Democrats were promoting Woodrow Wilson, the progressive governor of New Jersey. Running against him for re-election on the Republican ticket was president William Taft. To complicate the political scene, former president Theodore Roosevelt announced his candidacy on the Bull Moose ticket, so named after his statement that he felt "fit as a Bull Moose."

Jane Addams, Paul Kellogg, Owen Lovejoy and other well-known reformers had been made members of the Roosevelt platform committee. Though they objected to his militarism, they succeeded in incorporating into his domestic program the demands drawn up at a 1909 meeting of social workers which included woman suffrage, the abolition of child labor, and an eight-hour work day. Miss Addams, the most influential woman in the country, went on a speaking tour to promote Theodore Roosevelt for president. Again, the irony went unnoted that Miss Addams, who could not herself cast a vote, was nevertheless considered a key figure to get men to the polls. Her popularity alarmed the Wilson forces. To counteract her effectiveness, Jacob Schiff arranged with the Democratic National Committee to invite Lillian Wald to preside over their National Women's Organization and he himself pressured her to accept the position. "Mrs. Borden Harriman wishes me to urge you to take the presidency." She rejected the offer and Schiff's pressure as well, "because it would seem illogical for me, one who is a suffragette to assume official responsibility for a platform that repressed its plank." She continued, "I am not an aggressive suffragist but the issue is too real for one who had declared herself to have taken that position." She also begged off on grounds of ill health, writing her letters from Lake Placid. But Jacob Schiff did not easily back down. ". . . the social reforms for which you stand and labor need the support and confidence of the conservative classes . . . to which as an instance I myself belong . . ." If she and Jane Addams and Henry Moscowitz and others had succeeded in electing Roosevelt—what would Jacob Schiff have done?

It all faded into the ebb and flow of her experience. Schiff won that round with Woodrow Wilson's election. After her return to health and Henry Street, she thought ahead to the coming year which would mark twenty years of her work on the Lower East Side. In a lengthy letter, she presented Jacob Schiff with an elaborate plan for a celebration, outlining her ideas for a pageant that would present the contributions of the Henry Street Settlement and the Lower East Side to the vitality, culture, and growth of New York City.

─────10─────

Street Pageant

N E W S of a pageant in the spring of 1913 that would celebrate twenty years of the Henry Street Settlement and the Visiting Nurse Service spread through the city and brought volunteers flocking to headquarters. They wanted to share with Lillian Wald the satisfaction of being part of an institution, or a "personality," as some called the settlement.

The head resident had been honored the year before with an honorary degree of Doctor of Laws (LL.D.) bestowed by Mt. Holyoke College, and a medal from the National Institute of Social Sciences "for distinguished service to humanity." She had been a frequent visitor to the White House to advise Presidents Roosevelt and Taft on health matters.

As in the early days, Lillian Wald was being stretched to become more than she already was. She had grown into a prominent national figure, only to be drawn into the international arena when Henry Street was opened up as an educational institution for nurses from Africa, Asia, and Latin America, as well as Europe. In letters to distant lands she handed down guidelines that helped seed public health nursing in every corner of the world.

Standing at the pinnacle of her career, she held onto intertwining strands of work that laced through more than 100 organizations. She shrugged off the exhaustion brought on by her stewardship of countless responsibilities. Not for her such human frailties as fatigue when each day she faced anew a desk piled high with sheaves of paper for causes to be launched and work to be done.

When she was free to look back over the twenty years, she marveled at the level of achievement that grew out of her modest and even naïve beginnings, as if the single note she had sounded had developed into a chord and then into deeper harmonies. On the one hand she was driven to expand the parameters of her work and influence to guarantee the viability of her organizations. On the other, growth naturally evolved the way it did in other settlement houses, notably Hull House where tradition had been set for community work.

The year before she had decided, and Adelaide Nutting had agreed with her, that it was time to establish a National Organization of Public Health Nursing that would unite nurses and give them a stronger voice in politics. Wherever nurses gathered they credited Lillian Wald's vision for their improved status and increased self-esteem. Through expanded educational programs, new career openings, and an updated public image, she had helped professionalize nursing, calling her colleagues indispensable to the public health service. Further, she said, in a talk at Teachers College, "The nurse is a woman of rounded and self-balanced personality, creative, initiating ideas, able to lead, develop and direct her nursing service toward a goal of social betterment . . ." No longer, she said, is nursing a mere "handmaiden" but "a trusted and indispensable ally" to medical science in which "comradeship the physician gains as much as the nurse."

Her own settlement had become a large complex of seven buildings on Henry Street with branches on Sixtieth and Seventy-ninth streets. The boroughs of Manhattan and the Bronx had been districted to facilitate the work of ninety-two staff nurses who had made 200,000 home visits the year before. In crowded neighborhoods, she had rented three stores for milk stations and first-aid centers; brought about city inspection of midwives to eliminate unsanitary procedures; rented rooms at the Children's Aid Society for classes. She saw Henry Street catering to people from birth to old age; 3,000 were club members and more than 25,000 people used the settlement's facilities. "We are nearly bursting our walls," she proudly reported.

Most significant to her of all her contributions to public health was her success in keeping the family together. "Poor mothers with large families who cannot under any circumstances leave home to go to a hospital now receive all the attention that they need at home," she commented. She never lost her perception of her neighbors as individuals. They were ". . . men and women, old and young, with the strengths and weaknesses, the good and the bad, the appetites and wants that are common to us all . . ." she said in a talk on housing.

She herself found time to attend to the needs of the ordinary person. She ran uptown to the Hebrew Sheltering Society to see a troubled little boy, and then explained to Mr. Schiff, who chastised her for the needless expenditure of energy, "I cannot resist doing the best I can." Nor could she resist helping Maggie Lynch, who had been born with a stump for an arm, to which had grown a miniature hand. She used it to wring out clothes in the loft where she lived with her godmother, a hard working charwoman. When Maggie was sixteen and desperate to appear like everyone else, Miss Wald arranged to have her fitted with an artificial limb. On the day that the prosthesis was ready, Miss Wald accompanied Maggie to the manufacturer to be fitted. Underestimating the young girl's pride in the artificial limb, Miss Wald kept her eyes averted as they walked down the street in order not to embarrass her, only to hear Maggie stop every acquaintance and proudly display her new arm.

"Don't knock, just open the door and walk in," a woman shouted from her window to a visitor waiting to be admitted to the settlement. People meeting Miss Wald for the first time on the eve of the celebration would see a handsome woman of forty-six whose full face was framed by dark hair combed back from a broad brow. They would respond to her warm features, the wide mouth, soft and full-lipped, the flushed face, the wide apart brown eyes with lids drooping a bit along the outer edge. The smile, open and frank, would make every visitor an immediate friend. No longer the slender young woman of twenty years before, when nurse Georgia Beaver called her "a beautiful thing," she nevertheless carried her added weight gracefully. Inside the settlement she wore a nurse's blue uniform. Out on the street she was fashionably clothed in a long dress with a square neckline, long necklaces, and she always wore a hat. She could be hurrying to a meeting or a fund-raising event, greeting her neighbors on the way, a look of recognition in her eyes and smile; and she would say an endearing "hello" to youngsters on the street. One afternoon she was on her way to the upper East Side home of the Leo Arnsteins where women had been invited to tea to hear Miss Wald appeal for funds for scholarships for Henry Street's vocational guidance program. Any wealthy man or woman, interested in arranging a meeting of friends to make contributions to Henry Street, would have no trouble in doing so if it was known that Miss Wald herself would be the guest of honor.

As Jacob Schiff had predicted, she now headed such a large organization that she no longer personally knew all the nurses on her staff. Through levels of supervisory personnel she controlled the day-to-day functioning of the organization. Occasionally there were outbursts of anger at Miss Wald's dictatorial methods, for she held a tight grip over every aspect of work as if she were the sole designer of the intricate tapestry and others were only the weavers.

The top echelons at Henry Street were filled with the oldest residents, Ysabella Waters, Jane Hitchcock, Roberta Shatz, Helen McDowell, Harriet Knight, and others who had grown into administrative positions. There were also shifts within the "family" but always there was a handful of devoted residents to oversee the needs of the Lady.

"We can hardly understand how it is possible that you and your associates can do it all," Mr. Schiff wrote, alarmed at the inevitable increase in expense as her programs expanded. "What you ought *not* to do is to risk the incurrence of a considerable deficit which would likely personally plague you so much and so constantly that the work itself might become jeopardized. Your friends, and the friends of the work, among which I count myself with much gratification, need do everything to stand by you to enable a successful and un-diminished continuance of the great work done by you and your associates, but nevertheless you ought to consider whether some of the outside activities could not be diminished, in order that it shall be possible to maintain what, after all, is the main purpose and work of the Nurses' Settlement."

It was not the first time that he warned her about the increasing work and overhead, but it was like telling the rivers not to flow or the sea not to move with the tides. And so, disregarding his advice that she cut down on programs, she found a way of using the anniversary celebration as a fundraiser. She approached Mr. Schiff with the plan "to get an endowment for the Settlement. As you stated last winter," she wrote to him, "this effort would doubtless lead to people's remembering us in their wills as well . . . I do not want our Settlement to live one day longer than it deserves, . . . but I think that our work for the sick is analogous to the hospitals' acute and chronic, and that we ought not leave the thousand patients who now look to us entirely to the hazards of a precarious financial existence . . . You and Mrs. Loeb were the first friends and the first believers in me, and you have always made me feel that you are a sharer in every aspiration that I had for the safe-guarding and care of our sick . . . I have it in my heart to hope that you would be willing to take the leadership in a committee . . . for securing this endowment . . ."

How could Jacob Schiff turn her down? She continued to charm him and all her supporters. Those who became residents of Henry Street or who handled her legal and business affairs joined in the chorus of admiration. George W. Alger, her lawyer, would remark that Miss Wald was "an artist in the joy of living," and that he loved her "soundless chuckle." He would call Miss Wald "one of the most loved of the great women of our time." A. A. Berle, who started his public service career as a Henry Street resident, would say, "She was wonderful ... Everybody fell in love with Lillian Wald."

And it was for love of Lillian Wald as well as for the spectacle itself that 10,000 people would jam the streets to view the pageant and take part in the twentieth anniversary celebration of the Henry Street Settlement. Though she viewed Henry Street as a collective and requested that she personally was not to be honored, her colleagues found that impossible, for she was the architect of the monumental organization. Jacob Schiff had called her its soul.

Festivities started months before the pageant took place and continued into the fall with a public exhibition of the work of the organization. In January, Miss Wald started off the celebration by holding an afternoon meeting at which the mayor spoke for the city, Jacob Schiff for the directors, Florence Kelley for the residents, Rita Wallach Morgenthau for nonresidents, and finally Miss Wald, who outlined the achievements of the settlement.

Publicity brought gifts of money ranging from the twenty-five pennies given to a nurse by a newsboy to thousands of dollars contributed by the wealthy. A permanent committee was set up to insure regular salaries for nurses who were honored at a lavish dinner at the Park Avenue Hotel, sponsored jointly by the Nursing Education League and heads of nursing schools. Members of the American Hero Club and the Patriots Club and others, now successful men and women, put skills and money to use to smooth out program difficulties. At a special birthday celebration, the local library arranged an evening of stories of old New York. The city administration paved Henry Street for the occasion. Even the men of the fire department groomed their horses and polished brass-trimmed harnesses. The city police and sanitation departments gave their blessing by promising cooperation.

The pageant, which would become the forerunner of future New York City street festivals, had a cast of 500 under the direction of long-time volunteers Rita Wallach Morgenthau and Irene and Alice Lewisohn. In their club work they had produced dance and song programs to recreate traditions of ethnic groups. Irene Lewisohn, a student of ancient dance ritual, introduced free dance movement to music, made popular by Isadora Duncan. She achieved such a high level of artistry and authenticity in the productions she staged at Henry Street that they attracted an audience of uptown as well as local residents.

The pageant had as its theme the portrayal of the history of the region from its native residents to the flood of immigrants at the turn of the century. In the gymnasium, now spread out over the back rooms of three Henry Street buildings, small boys and girls had rehearsed how to be Manhata Indians, the region's original residents. In clubs and schools, older children practiced the traditional songs and dances of the various national groups that made up the neighborhood. The first arrived, the Dutch, were shown dancing around the Maypole. Polkas and ballads of the 1860s portrayed the mid-century. And the final fifty years were brought to life in choral songs and dances of the Irish, Scottish, German, Italian, and Russian immigrants.

For months volunteers had dug into archives to find these old songs and dances. Young club members became apprentices to artists and carpenters designing and building sets; to lighting experts planning the use of spots. They worked as painters, plasterers, and decorators. The old church down the street was draped in flags; the school provided rehearsal space; and the library opened its stacks to researchers.

Behind the scenes, wealthy contributors arranged teas and dinners to raise funds. Active in committee work were social leaders Mrs. Bernard Gimbel, Miss Harriet de Puy, Mrs. Emmons Blaine, Mrs. Butler Duncan, and Miss Catherine Bliss.

And day after day, in a small flat belonging to Henry Street resident Harriet Knight and borrowed for the occasion, were Rita Wallach Morgenthau and her uptown friends Aline Bernstein and her sister, Ethel Frankau.

Mrs. Bernstein came each day from her brownstone carrying lunch in a paper bag packed by her maid. She and her sister designed costumes for 500 pageant participants and supervised a corps of neighborhood men, women, and older children who came to the flat in the evenings to sew seams and stitch hems. Each period costume was authentic, for the women prided themselves on their historical research. Their skills made it possible to make each costume at the budgeted allotment of fifty cents. Work on the pageant initiated the sisters as Henry Street volunteers, and they later went on to successful creative careers—Mrs. Bernstein became an outstanding theatrical costume and set designer, and Ethel Frankau made her mark in the fashion industry.

During the two evenings of the pageant in June people hung from rooftops, crowded against tenement windows, and fought for space on stoops. Miss Wald launched festivities on the sixth of June with a small dinner at Henry Street for her wealthy supporters. Much in evidence were Jacob Schiff and his wife, Theresa, the Paul Warburgs, the Leo Arnsteins, Court Justice Samuel Greenbaum, Borough President of Manhattan George McAneny, the financial wizard and philanthropist V. Everit Macy, Charles R. Crane from Chicago, and others. After dinner, they joined 350 honored guests seated on a block-long grandstand around which twinkled a thousand electric lights.

The pealing of church bells announced the opening of the pageant and the first contingent filed out of the nearby school, and paraded down the street to greet Lillian Wald standing in front of her home at 265 Henry Street. They then marched to the grandstand and the spectacle unfolded, recreating the life of the region. The final contingent, made up of uniformed Visiting Nurses of Henry Street in starched blue uniforms, brought another salvo of cheers and the church bells again rang out mingling with the clamor. Jacob Riis called the pageant a symbol of the rebirth of "the whole crowded, suffering, once-forgotten East Side." The homage of the entire city was paid to Lillian Wald in this celebration of twenty years of her work.

In the aftermath came a letter from Jacob Schiff lauding the pageant and "the warm-hearted tributes paid to you, and perhaps last but not least in the pride those of your up-town friends took—including ourselves—that they had the opportunity to take part in the celebration and in the triumphs . . . of the work and methods of the Henry Street Settlement. God bless you and hold you in his keeping!

"The enclosed holiday gift may be appropriated in such manner as you may yourself deem best . . . With Mrs. Schiff's and my own loving greetings to you and the entire Henry Street family."

For Lillian Wald, whose triumphs reverberated through the summer months of that year into the fall, there were pleasures and petty frustrations. To Rita Wallach Morgenthau she expressed her regret that "credit for organizing the pageant [in the *New York Times*] was not given to you, that Jane Hitchcock's name and Ysabella Waters's were left out . . . [as was] Mrs. Harkness who gives more money than any one person . . . [but she] will not give a rap!"

The success of the celebration eased her way. She saw a glorious future ahead, one in which she would be able to continue the pace and direction of her work. In the White House, President Wilson spoke of "justice, liberty, and peace."

"I am aware that the world is full of love," she wrote to Rita Wallach Morgenthau in March, 1914, while on vacation in Jamaica, "and that we (you and I and all of us) have the most wonderful share in spreading the gospel of love and faith and work that ever was. I am almost ashamed to be such a millionaire."

But in the wings were new events, eruptions of violence in Europe that would force her onto a new course. In June, 1914, pistol shots killed an archduke and his wife in the Serbian town of Sarajevo. By the end of July, European nations divided into two hostile camps and declared war on each other. By August 2, the first shots were fired in "the bloodiest war ever fought on earth," as reported in the *New York Times*. By the end of August France had lost 100,000 men, countries had been invaded, and atrocity stories about the murder of civilians rolled off the presses.

In the United States the beginnings of World War I aroused peace advocates into immediate and dramatic action, turning Lillian Wald into an outspoken leader of the antimilitarist forces.

—11—

Marching for Peace

M I S S Wald was on vacation in Woods Hole, Massachusetts, when she received a telegram. "We unanimously ask that you lead [an antiwar] parade. Please do not refuse . . ." When finally she wired agreement, an enthusiastic follow-up letter came from Lillian Deaver, in charge of arrangements, apologizing for interrupting Miss Wald's vacation and ending with "God bless you, dear Miss Wald. I wish there were more of you in our big city." Miss Wald made only one request, that Mrs. Fanny Garrison Villard, a militant pacifist and daughter of abolitionist William Lloyd Garrison, be asked to chair the parade committee.

Thus Miss Wald affiliated with women activists in New York City who had hastily banded together to express their opposition to war and their solidarity with the women of Europe. They thought at first only of an immediate demonstration of their antiwar feelings and took their protest to the streets. On August 29, 1914, one month after the outbreak of World War I, New York City saw its first peace parade.

Fifteen hundred women silently marched down Fifth Avenue to

the beat of muffled drums. A platoon of mounted police walked their horses at the head of the line, followed by a young woman carrying the only flag, a white peace banner of a dove and olive branch. Mrs. Villard marched after her. Miss Wald followed in the first line of honored guests whom she knew from social work, labor, and the reform movement. Among them were Mary E. Dreier, Rose Schneiderman, and Leonora O'Reilly of the Women's Trade Union League; author and leading feminist Charlotte Perkins Gilman; suffragists Anna Howard Shaw and Carrie Chapman Catt. And then came line after line of women: pacifists, socialists, trade unionists, and women of warring nations—German, English, Austrian, French—marching side by side. They were dressed in black for mourning; those in white wore black armbands. Present was every shade of political and religious opinion and every age group—young mothers wheeling baby carriages, the frail elderly in five automobiles provided for them. There was a contingent of black women and a group of Henry Street nurses clad in blue uniforms.

Twenty thousand spectators lined the streets and thousands more crowded office building windows, silently looking on. In a sympathetic article, the *New York Herald* carried a front page story over a photograph of the parade, calling it "an impressive protest against war made by mothers, wives, and daughters in this city."

But war propaganda was also claiming newspaper headlines: ENGLAND'S CRY FOR FIGHTING MEN. LONDON CHEERS THE MEN WHO ARE GOING TO WAR. In photographs depicting the destruction of peaceful Belgium by invading German armies, the first atrocity stories fanned the ardor of militaristic cliques.

In personal letters to friends in the United States, English pacifists wrote of their despair. Decades of work had gone up in flames by the sudden destructive force of war. "I wish I were dead," wrote humanist philosopher Lowes Dickinson. Others wanted to fall into a deep sleep until the war was over.

Miss Wald had been involved in her usual pursuits when war struck Europe. The month before she had testified before the U.S. Commission on Industrial Relations on conditions in the garment industry; in June she had spoken on the need to enforce labor laws in tenements; she met with members of the boys clubs to encourage fundraising for their own building which would house a library, gymnasium, and game rooms. She had finally signed a contract with a publisher for a book on the founding of Henry Street titled *House on Henry Street* and discovered the writing of her memoirs was surprisingly satisfying. It was a splendid period for her, confirming her faith in democracy, especially when President Woodrow Wilson carried out campaign promises for domestic reform. Everywhere organizations had sprung up proclaiming peace as essential to such progress. There was an American Peace Society, and church, labor, and socialist peace groups. Millions of club women spoke out for peace. A few years before, steel magnate Andrew Carnegie had endowed a peace foundation with a ten-million-dollar contribution. Woodrow Wilson himself said he was a man for peace.

Growing out of Miss Wald's work in the community was her personal vision of the future. She had helped people of different national origins and religions live and work together. Christian and Jew, young and old, had built a community. That same cooperative spirit, she believed, could transcend frontiers and unite in common humanity people of all lands. Disagreements would be mediated in a world court and a spirit of cooperation and peace would prevail.

On her trip to Japan in 1910, she had admired the insignia people wore to identify family members. A Japanese artist, at her request, created an emblem for Henry Street which meant "we are all one family," or "Universal Brotherhood." She had that insignia imprinted on letterheads and publications.

The unleashing of war in Europe, violent and coercive, was shattering her dream. She could not stand it. War is a "demon of destruction and a hideous wrong—murder devastating home and happiness," she said with unaccustomed passion.

Lillian Wald was not alone in her fear that the European war would drag the United States into battle. Women were the first to respond to the dangers. They cried out that war's violent destruction was an obsolete way to settle grievances. Their acculturation as healers and nurturers gave them special understanding of pacifist women in warring countries, and they called for international solidarity. It is a crime to send sons and husbands out to be slaughtered, said Mrs. Villard. "Women must be trained to realize what the enormity of war is."

Jacob Schiff made publicly known his position for peace. In an interview in the *New York Times* he said that if peace came with the victory of one country over another and the dictation of peace terms by the victor, it would "only be a harbinger of another war." Known to Miss Wald was his personal grief of having one nephew in the British army and another fighting with the Germans.

Acting as a committee of three, Lillian Wald, Jane Addams, and Paul Kellogg, editor of the popular social work magazine, the *Survey*, called a meeting at Henry Street of labor, reform, and social work leaders to launch antiwar actions. Thus, a politically advanced group of leaders, experienced in mass action and public relations, activated the peace movement, removing it from clubrooms to give it wide exposure. In a series of round-table discussions, the coalition was joined by long-time reform leaders Rabbi Stephen S. Wise of the Free Synagogue; John Haynes Holmes of the Community Church; Emily Greene Balch, professor of economics at Wellesley College; Edward T. Devine of the School of Philanthropy; Florence Kelley; Alice Lewisohn; Crystal Eastman; a lawyer and radical activist; Amos Pinchot and Max Eastman of *Masses* magazine, a periodical of social protest; Norman Thomas, then a pastor of the East Harlem Church; author Zona Gale; and other professionals and social workers.

By the second meeting, the coalition issued a statement condemning war which "has brought low our conception of the preciousness of human life as slavery brought low our conception of human liberty." It pointed to the abuse of the word "patriotism" and the cruelty and brutishness that prevailed in wartime and set "faithful against faithful, priest against priest, put its stamp on growing children teaching them to hate other children; whetted a lust for profits."

After various stages of organization, the coalition emerged in 1915 as the Anti-Preparedness Committee and in 1916 as the American Union Against Militarism (AUAM). Lillian Wald agreed to serve as president of the executive board; Crystal Eastman became executive secretary. The organization "opposed the principles and practices of militarism because they threaten the institutions essential to democracy." And it was for her faith in democracy that Lillian Wald undertook taxing new responsibilities. Her leadership of the antiwar organization commanded a wide range of liberal and even conservative support.

Still, leading an antiwar organization was not the same as fighting to feed undernourished children. Woman, the nurturer, could stand up in the forefront of the fight for social welfare. Peace was different. It took the struggle into mined waters. To begin with, there was the confrontation with an erstwhile friend, former president Theodore Roosevelt, who had warmed his feet at her fireplace and for whom she had campaigned in 1912. At that time he had subdued his bellicosity, but with the first shot of gunfire in Europe he roared for a U.S. military build-up and became the acknowledged leader of the promilitary forces.

Her commitment to peace cut into other responsibilities but she weighed the sacrifices she had to make "to save the very soul of our nation," as she would put it. Nor did she accept the office as an honorary post only to rubber-stamp decisions. She assumed an active role in the leadership of the AUAM, making it clear that the organization would function "within friendly government relations."

Peace was then a popular cause and to Miss Wald's way of thinking she was building a body of articulate support for President Wilson's peace statements. Her organization would "campaign against preparedness, support the government's neutrality position and plan for a world federation of nations to guarantee world peace."

Her faith in the president was bolstered when in mid-December, 1914, he sent his top aide, Colonel Edward House, to the belligerent nations to initiate peace negotiations. Though the negotiations failed Miss Wald was convinced she had a friend in the White House. Indeed, the president further substantiated Miss Wald's confidence when he called her, Jane Addams, Paul Kellogg, Rabbi Wise, Reverend Holmes, and other liberal peace leaders to his office for an informal exchange of views.

She was unequivocal about matters connected to the war. By early November, 1914, she was asked by Miss Crandall, head of the Public Nurse Association, what she thought about the humanitarian requests for nurses coming from abroad, especially from war-torn Belgium. In a forthright reply, Miss Wald reminded Miss Crandall that her position had already been stated, as had Lavinia Dock's, in the *American Journal of Nursing*. Miss Wald continued:

> War is war! We who hate it, who would make every sacrifice . . . to prevent it . . . must guard every act that we do, every impulse that moves us, to discover whether directly or indirectly we are supporting war . . . I think we must acknowledge that when we send relief, surgeons and nurses . . . to the fields of battle, we are to some extent perpetuating, and, in a way, glorifying war and its barbarisms.

> I also believe that when people's emotions are stirred to feel the heroism of giving relief on the battlefield, unconsciously they glorify and make heroic all that happens on the battlefield . . .

> Time was when war seemed to be inevitable . . . That time we thought had passed. This European war shatters more than the people who are maimed for life or the homes that are laid waste.

And then she added that she hoped women were taking their individual responsibility for peace more seriously.

Thus began for Miss Wald a sequence of activities that fullfilled the bold initiative of August when she had led the peace march down Fifth Avenue. Instinctively she knew the organic connection between peace and social reform, and as the war clouds cast by the European war grew more threatening, she feared that the era of progressive change might come to an end. It was worth her best efforts to keep her country on a safe course.

To build up every available force in opposition to the war, she joined thousands of women at the New Willard Hotel in Washington, D.C., for the formation of the Woman's Peace Party in January, 1915. Inspiration had come from two European women, outstanding peace activists and suffragists, whose countries were at war: Rosika Schwimmer, a Hungarian, and Emmeline Pethick-Lawrence, an Englishwoman.

In the first years of World War I, the woman's suffrage movement contributed its expertise to the antiwar fight. Carrie Chapman Catt, head of the National Woman Suffrage Association, chaired the founding meeting of the Woman's Peace Party in Washington. Jane Addams was elected national chairman. The *New York Times* reported the meeting as an effort to "enlist all American women to arouse the nation to respect the sacredness of human life and to abolish war."

The organization in a forceful preamble urged women to recognize their united power, to seize the moment and help shape the destiny of the country. Not only should they do so because they were women, "especially the custodians of the life of the ages; . . . charged with the future of childhood," but also because they must demand the right to share political decision making. ". . . we will no longer consent to its [life's] reckless destruction . . . We demand that women be given a share in deciding between war and peace in all the courts of high debate—within the home, the school, the church, the industrial order, and the state." In this powerful leap forward women abandoned their inferior status to demand equality on every level. In a sense such a demand acknowledged the powerful positions women like Lillian Wald, Jane Addams, Florence Kelley, and many others had already achieved. The discreet roles they played— respectable ladies tagging after men's leadership—masked their true strength.

The Woman's Peace Party set up a New York branch headed by Crystal Eastman and Ruth Pickering (Mrs. Amos) Pinchot. It launched its activity with the statement, "Women are saying they will not bear sons to be slaughtered."

Miss Wald, queried by suffrage leader Alice Stone Blackwell (niece of Dr. Elizabeth Blackwell) about whether she thought wars would be less frequent if women voted, replied, "I believe that women would be less willing to vote large sums for armaments . . . they were temperamentally less stimulated than men by the call to force . . ."

Miss Wald and other peace leaders allied themselves with the pacifists of warring countries who had courageously launched peace initiatives. Dr. Aletta Jacobs, a Dutch suffrage leader and pioneer physician, urged women to cut across boundaries and meet to discuss war and peace. As head of the organizing committee for such a meeting, she asked Jane Addams to preside over a conference at The Hague, in the Netherlands.

Thus Jane Addams led a delegation of forty-five U.S. delegates to a peace conference in the Netherlands, in April, 1915, ten months after the start of the European conflict. "Dearest Lady," Lillian Wald wrote to Jane Addams explaining why she could not be a delegate, "It would seriously affect [my] usual responsibilities . . . that I cannot properly abandon. I will see you off on the 13th of April."

On that day Miss Wald went down to the pier in Hoboken, New Jersey, where the Dutch ship *Noordam* was berthed, a white flag emblazoned with the word PEACE in blue, flying from its mast. Her disappointment in not being able to join the group of distinguished women sailing with Miss Addams deepened as she greeted many old friends among the delegates: Dr. Alice Hamilton, Professor Emily Greene Balch, Grace Abbot, director of the Immigration Protective League, Professor Sophonisba Breckinridge of the University of Chicago, Madeleine Z. Doty of the Women's Lawyers Associations, trade union leader Leonora O'Reilly, Annie E. Molloy of the Telephone Operators Union, and Louis Lochner, head of the Chicago Peace Society, who traveled with the delegation as secretary. Among the delegates was Mabel Hyde Kittredge, whom Miss Wald had appointed unofficial representative of Henry Street.

Miss Addams set the tone for the conference, declaring before the ship sailed, "We do not think we can settle the war . . . We do think it is valuable to state a new point of view. We do think it is fitting that women should meet and take counsel and see what may be done."

After waving the delegates off, Miss Wald returned to the city to face a hostile press, gleefully reporting Theodore Roosevelt's ridicule of the delegates. He called them "silly and base" and "influenced by physical cowardice."

Miss Wald was kept informed of the ocean crossing and conference proceedings through Miss Kittredge's letters. It was a "thrilling experience," Miss Kittredge wrote, to meet in workshops aboard ship three times each day to discuss peace proposals with brilliant women, especially with Miss Addams as leader. Despite government interference that prevented the English delegates from crossing the mined waters of the North Sea to get to The Hague and an acrimonious European press that alternated between attacks on and ridicule of the pacifists, the public sessions at the conference drew crowds of 2,000.

Jane Addams, elected chair of the International Congress, called The Hague conference "a precious moment in human experience," and saw the journey of delegates from war-torn nations as nothing short of "an act of heroism."

Back home, Miss Wald worked with a committee of peace women to set up elaborate plans to welcome the delegates' return. New York newspapers had given wide coverage to the controversial actions of the conference, especially to its dramatic decision to send delegations to both neutral and warring nations to urge continuous mediation until a just armistice was brought about.

In an especially courageous action, Jane Addams headed a mission of women to belligerent countries (both allies and central powers). On May 7, 1915, she was meeting with British government officials when the Germans torpedoed and sank the British ship *Lusitania*. Two hundred American passengers were among the thousand who lost their lives. "Treasonable," the press called Miss Addams's point of view, talking peace instead of urging an all-out war against a brutal, tyrannical Germany!

In the United States, the sinking of the *Lusitania* bolstered prowar forces who increased their clamour for preparedness. A stream of books and articles complained of U.S. military and naval weakness. And Hollywood-produced motion pictures portrayed invasions by a German-style enemy. Reflecting this turn in direction, President Wilson veered off on a new course and by July, 1915, had come out for preparedness. "The president was sowing the seeds of militarism," said Oswald Garrison Villard.

In the midst of this outpouring of propaganda, Miss Wald

sounded a solemn note at Henry Street's July Fourth Liberty Festival to celebrate the Declaration of Independence. Calling it both a "joyous and a solemn day," she said, "The American people made up of the blood of all nations best comprehend that there is no real hatred among them . . . that the real thing [is] true and deep devotion to the principles of democracy, the preservation of life and liberty and unalterable opposition to war and destruction, to the insane tearing down of civilization."

War propaganda was still in its early stages when Jane Addams and the peace delegates returned home in mid-July, 1915. At the pier to greet them was Lillian Wald and a committee of sixty women. Accompanied by two others, Miss Wald took a cutter down the bay to board the *St. Louis*, on which the women had sailed. After brief ceremonies at the pier, Miss Wald and Miss Addams drove to Henry Street where Miss Wald had arranged a luncheon for personal friends.

A Carnegie Hall meeting a few days later heard Miss Addams propose her central theme. She spoke of "a council of neutral nations" to meet and remain in continuous session, in order to provide a channel of mediation for belligerents to negotiate an end to the war. The United States, Miss Addams said, was the logical country to initiate such a procedure. Straightforward in her attack on war and its needless slaughter, she reported to the audience that she had heard the same complaint in all belligerent nations: "this war was an old man's war, that the young men who were dying . . . were not the men who wanted war, and were not the men who believed in war."

To counteract the popularity of the antiwar women, a pro-preparedness woman's organization was launched in August, 1915, called the Special Relief Society. Encouraged by such militarists as Theodore Roosevelt, a group of society women announced they were giving up "bridge and embroidery" and social undertakings in order to train for war. In the event of an invasion they did not wish to be caught defenseless the way Belgium had been.

An enterprising newspaperman, who found the polarization among women intriguing, interviewed Miss Wald and a group of pacifists at a luncheon at the Women's University Club. Miss Wald opposed war preparation calling it counter to President Wilson's wish that everyone remain calm. Lavinia Dock stated, "If war was something which fell upon the human race from the skies like hail, I could understand these ladies and think they were very prudent and wise. But as war comes about solely by and through the actions of human individuals and therefore can be avoided by them, I confess I do not understand their point of view."

By the end of 1915, the president began an odd strategy of talking peace and preparing for war as he supported moves for "the greatest U.S. Navy in the World." In a Flag Day parade in Washington, D.C., he appeared with an American flag draped across his chest. He is "joyriding with the jingoes," said Secretary of State William Jennings Bryan of the president.

The peace forces, in a steady barrage of telegrams and letters to the White House, urged a conference to end the war. At the end of 1915, they mobilized behind the Ford Peace Ship, a project financed by automobile industrialist Henry Ford, a consistent peace advocate. Ford, and those behind him, proposed to send a peace delegation to a neutral Scandinavian port to meet with Europeans to work out a peace program. But infighting and confusion mired the project before it got started. Jane Addams, ill with pneumonia, called off her participation and was accused by the press of feigning a nervous breakdown. Although the *Louis II* sailed in December, 1915, carrying abroad journalists and peace delegates, it did not accomplish its mission.

By the beginning of 1916, pacifists were being attacked in the press. The *New Jersey Herald* called them "Serious enemies of the Republic, honest as they may be in their opinions."

Carrying on antiwar work as well as a round of fund-raising activities, Miss Wald took advantage of the publication of her book, *House on Henry Street*, to attend a celebration at the Schiffs where she talked to a hundred guests about her community programs. Other events demanded her attention, such as a dinner at Rabbi Wise's Free Synagogue in honor of Henry Morgenthau, a dedicated Henry Street supporter who had been appointed U.S. Ambassador to Turkey.

Increasing war propaganda put Miss Wald and other antimilitarists on the alert, forcing them to move ahead with more articles in magazines and newspapers and more frequent meetings. In an artticle, "Seeing Red," Miss Wald warned, "When militarism comes in at the door, democracy flies out of the window." Welfare programs were already being shelved by government expenditure of its revenues for militaristic purposes. "A wave of hysteria is sweeping over the country under the seemingly reasonable name of 'preparedness,'" she said. "But it has a sinister resemblance to the shadow of European militarism . . ." And it was a "perilous threat to democracy . . . When you put a gun into a man's hand you give him the best argument for shooting."

In February, 1916, she was headlined as one of the WARNING VOICES AGAINST PREPAREDNESS in the *New York Post.* When she and Florence Kelley testified before the House and Senate Military Affairs Committee, the *Post* described them this way: "Next to Jane Addams it would be hard to find two women who are more devoted patriots and are working longer hours for the advancement of America every day in the year than Lillian Wald and Florence Kelley."

Miss Wald, who acted as marshal of the antipreparedness speakers in the afternoon session, said, "We are anxious to have you realize that we are a group of ordinary, thoughtful American citizens, determined to look at the situation calmly, with reason— wisely if we can . . . The President hints at great dangers . . . but the American people want to know what they are. They have reason to fear secret diplomacy, an inevitable corollary to militaristic domination, and we are all warned by our English friends that secret diplomacy at home is more to be feared than an enemy abroad."

Faced with an increasing momentum toward preparedness, and a press that was partial to war propaganda, Lillian Wald, Crystal Eastman, and the AUAM leadership, indefatigable and creative, broadened the organization by putting to work every known strategy to maintain its public visibility. Initially they represented peace positions ranging from pacifism to militant socialism. But when the revolutionary poet John Reed, socialist leader Allan Benson, and St. Louis social worker Roger Baldwin joined their ranks, they acquired a more outspoken group. Everyone against war marched behind the AUAM banner, the most powerful peace organization in the country. It carried its message through chapters in twenty-two cities, a paying membership of over 3,000, and tens of thousands of supporters. Its antiwar literature, speakers, and mass meetings educated the public to facts and figures about munitions makers, profits, and the need for world peace.

To counteract President Wilson's stepped-up war talk in a tour of the country, the AUAM launched its own "Truth about Preparedness" campaign by sending speakers to eleven cities. Miss Wald gave the keynote address to the packed-to-the-doors Carnegie Hall meeting on April 6, 1916, that launched the tour. She stood on a dais beneath a banner draped across the stage, DEMOCRACY VERSUS MILITARISM. And in her reasonable, moderated voice she denounced the military build-up and war propaganda as "a great peril to the America that has the passionate love of its patriots . . . Militarism has invaded us from every side and even marched into our schools . . . to establish conscription. Extraordinary and unprecedented measures have been taken to promote a public demand for military and naval expansion, and these have brought in their train hysteria and the camp followers of self interest. Fear has dethroned reason and people are seeing things at night . . ."

Mr. Schiff, concerned about her increasing fatigue, wrote, "You are all too negligent of your health, which is wrong in general and moreover bad economics, and I am also afraid that in some things you are incorrigible!" To which Miss Wald, annoyed, replied, "I really am not incorrigible and am doing the best I can. I would not have gone to the meeting at Carnegie Hall last night if it had seemed at all fair to keep away. I left after my little speech and I don't think it hurt me."

She was provoked into ceaseless activity when the next day she read a newspaper column about the Carnegie Hall meeting and next to it an article about the escalating war drive with a headline announcing BIG CONCERNS TO AID MILITARY TRAINING. It read: "Fifty banking and business houses will pay salaries of workers while at camps. The cost will be two million dollars."

The might of industry, banking, and other conservative forces combined into a formidable prowar lobby. And as the United States increased its munitions exports to the allies, boosting employment to an all-time high, the rank and file of the labor movement began to go soft on the war.

The changing public attitudes made the president reluctant to meet with the antimilitarists, and specifically with Miss Wald. "What do you think of this? It seems to me literally impossible . . . to have these people come and make speeches to me," he wrote to his aide Joseph Tumulty. But Tumulty replied, he did "not see how the president [could] turn Miss Wald down."

She headed a delegation to see the president after the May, 1916, passage of the National Defense Act, which broadened the power of the government in the militarization of the country. Her delegation urged the president to call a conference of neutral nations to end the war. Some of the delegates found that the president's position had suffered a moral decline. Miss Wald, however, maintained her faith in Mr. Wilson. "We know at heart he is an anti-militarist," she said, but "we are particularly fearful of . . . introducing military training in the public schools . . . and an effort to stampede the country into militarism." To meet the changing public attitudes, the AUAM bent its position and came out for "sane and reasonable preparedness."

In the meantime, tensions with Mexico increased and the threat of war was closer to home. Matters came to a head in March, 1916, when General Pershing headed a punitive expedition of 6,000 armed men. They penetrated 300 miles deep into Mexico in pursuit of Pancho Villa, the Mexican revolutionary. The Mexican people raised an uproar at the invasion of their land by a foreign country.

A bloody incident in the town of Carrizal, where Mexicans and Americans fired at each other killing soldiers on both sides, almost brought a declaration of war by the United States. The AUAM, inspired by Crystal Eastman's and Lillian Wald's firm leadership, met in emergency session at the home of Alice Lewisohn. There they decided to take ads in leading newspapers to reprint the report of a U.S. officer that U.S. soldiers had provoked the incident. At the same time they launched a telephone and telegram campaign to Washington urging the government to remain calm. Three of their members, including David Starr Jordan, retired president of Stanford University, became part of an unofficial mediating body to adjudicate the controversy. The success of the undertaking prompted the AUAM to emphasize the importance of masses of people in bringing about a peaceful solution to a war threat. Perhaps only the people would be able to end the European war.

By the summer of 1916, Miss Wald was ailing and forced to leave her round-the-clock work for a rest in New Hampshire. But there was no refuge from newspaper headlines and the sweep toward the United States's preparedness. How could she rest when the stakes were so high? Death and destruction had changed the face of Europe; two and a half million men had been killed in two and a half years of fighting. Families were destroyed; millions were homeless; countries had become a wasteland where once there were farms and cities.

After a brief rest, Lillian Wald was back at her desk and quickly caught up in the presidential election of 1916. Woodrow Wilson was running for re-election against Republican candidate Charles Evans Hughes, now a justice of the U.S. Supreme Court, and backed by Theodore Roosevelt and the promilitary forces. Wilson had come out for a strong progressive domestic program, advocating reforms he had never before supported, such as an eight-hour day for railroad workers and a National Child Labor bill for which Lillian Wald and Florence Kelley were still fighting. Nevertheless, Miss Wald, Jane Addams, and other peace advocates withheld their endorsement of Wilson. In September, when Democratic campaign managers urged Miss Wald to declare her support, she suggested it was a good time for the president to make a statement about conscription, then being discussed in Congress. The president, eager to reaffirm his peace image, wrote to Lillian Wald assuring her that conscription should rest with Congress and not with the executive branch of government.

Wilson's campaign presented him as a man of peace. A barrage of publicity hammered away at slogans such as "He Kept Us Out of War" and "Internationalism abroad and Progressivism at home." A party advertisement offered the dire choice between HUGHES, ROOSEVELT AND WAR or WILSON AND PEACE WITH HONOR. To millions in urban centers, across the prairies, and in the Far West, who yearned for peace, and who feared the imperialistic policies of Hughes, Wilson emerged as the only choice. He drew his support from social workers, reform activists, liberals, and pockets of radicals who defected from their parties to campaign for him. Lillian Wald found herself surrounded by new allies such as John Reed, Lincoln Steffens, Norman Hapgood, Max Eastman, and hundreds of others usually associated with radical causes. Opposing Wilson were Eugene Debs, Oswald Garrison Villard, the radical wing of the Socialist party, and the radical suffragists, among them Lavinia Dock, who denounced Wilson's refusal to back a federal suffrage amendment.

Wilson, in those hectic months, seemed to shrink further into himself, appearing thinner, taller, stilled by greater tension, his hair flattened on his small head, steel-rimmed pince-nez riding high across the bridge of his nose. To Miss Wald he remained a heroic figure, a peace advocate and idealist. She saw no alternative to supporting him. Militant politics that had within them the seeds of violence and hatred frightened her. By nature she was a mediator, a moderate, convinced that good could be found in every person, that no one was worthy of hate. It was far easier for her to use personal persuasion or moral force, far easier to persevere in her faith in President Wilson and his promise to maintain peace than to seek a radical option.

Wilson squeaked to victory with a narrow margin, a victory for which the AUAM and the reform movement generally took credit. When in December, 1916, he issued another call to warring nations offering mediation, Miss Wald felt justified in her faith in him. The peace offer came too late, for the belligerents were locked in a bitter conflict that only a military victory would end.

After the election, Miss Wald again shifted position, writing to the AUAM education director, Charles T. Hallinan, that "it would be wise not to swing too hard upon 'No Preparedness' for this is too remote a hope for realization at the present time."

Her perceptions were accurate, for by early 1917 the years of prowar rumblings erupted into sweeping war preparation. Wilson still spoke about "peace without victory," but events moved out of his grasp when on January 31, Germany announced the resumption of submarine warfare, then torpedoed U.S. merchant vessels. That decision by Germany brought into the open the support the United States had been giving the Allies. Martial spirit enflamed the country as if only in war and death there was honor.

The AUAM alone telegraphed Wilson that the United States should "refuse to allow herself to be dragooned into war . . ." These telegrams appeared as advertisements in the popular press signed by Lillian Wald, Emily Greene Balch, a professor of economics at Wellesley, Crystal Eastman, Oswald Garrison Villard, and others.

On February 3, the United States broke off diplomatic relations with Germany. Three weeks later Wilson called for the arming of merchant vessels. "Our heart is with the President," Miss Wald wired the White House. "His friends hardly sleep at night or rest by day in their ardent desire to help him sustain his high moral plane and to keep us out of war." The AUAM supported "armed neutrality."

She hardly slept at night, wrestling with conflict. She and friends walked a tightrope as they tried to figure out how to oppose war yet support the president in what they called his moral dilemma. Exhausting days, indeed. She had backed "armed neutrality," but others in the AUAM opposed her. An active board member, Dr. James A. Warbasse, claimed "armed neutrality was a compromise with war." Wilson was dangerous, he said, because "he proceeds to war with peacelike speeches."

A hastily formed new peace committee, the Emergency Peace Federation, headed by Emily Greene Balch, sent a delegation to meet with President Wilson on February 28. Lillian Wald and the others came away convinced that war was inevitable. In effect they received advance notice of the president's changed course. By March 15, the overthrow of the Russian tsar by a coalition of forces under

Alexandr Kerensky had edged the United States still closer to the war so it might bolster the allies in the event Russia withdrew her armies.

But the United States was still polarized and restless. Labor threatened strikes, especially against the railroads; and the foreign born, the German nationals in particular, loomed as a specter of disloyalty who, said the president, would be "crushed" if they acted treasonably. Fear possessed people's minds and reportings of German submarines off the coast, of bombs in locker rooms and under tables, made press headlines. "Americanism" became the patriotic word. In its name vituperation spilled out against the foreign born (hyphenated Americans, the president called them). A militaristic wave surged across the nation, unleashing lunatic passions determined to whip the opposition into line. In the deluge, the effectiveness of the antimilitarists was brought to low ebb by major defections.

Within the first three months of 1917, Carrie Chapman Catt "offered the services of the suffragists in case the United States went to war." Rabbi Stephen Wise, after much introspection, resigned from the executive board of the AUAM, for he had had a dramatic change of heart, and saw in the prowar forces the only legitimate way to throttle "the greater evil," German militarism. His defection shocked the antimilitarists. But he was not alone. Jacob Schiff also knew which side his heart was on. It was with his country and he floated war bonds to help the United States war effort. Henry Ford gave his factory to the government and offered to turn out submarines and motors without profit. Old friends and settlement house leaders Paul Kellogg, Mary Simkhovitch, and Robert Woods supported the United States entry into war. American Socialists split, many joining the war effort as did academicians and reformers William English Walling, Upton Sinclair, and Rose Pastor Stokes. The Carnegie Peace Endowment announced it would serve the ideal of its founder best by helping to bring the war to a successful conclusion. From pulpit, school, and street corner arose a fever for war. March 11 was "War Sunday" in New York churches. Samuel Gompers, head of the AFL, pledged labor's support, though the United Mine Workers stood firmly opposed. Pacifists were labeled "traitors" and antiwar congressmen were burned in effigy. To quote the writer Randolph Bourne, who remained a pacifist, "They lay down and floated with the current."

There was a rush to be with the majority. For to stand alone for peace brought dread isolation and abuse, hooligan attacks, the sneers and demonic rage of a mad fringe who in the name of patriotism created new myths and vented violence on the innocent. Torn asunder were old friendships and an old unity.

Standing grimly opposed to the country's pitiless sweep toward war were Lillian Wald, Jane Addams, Crystal Eastman, Emily Greene Balch, and a handful of others. They mounted an emergency campaign hopeful they could stem the implacable tide. They sent retired president of Stanford University David Starr Jordan on a speaking tour. In Baltimore, a mob of 1,000 broke into the hall where he appeared and forced their way toward the platform. Only the audience, standing up as one to sing the national anthem, brought the hoodlums to a standstill until Mr. Jordan could be spirited out of the hall. The next day, packs of vigilantes roamed the streets searching for him singing, "We'll hang Dave Jordan to a sour apple tree," while he stayed safely sheltered at the home of a friend.

WAR IS NOT NECESSARY, headlined a full-page ad placed in the leading newspapers, a last-ditch effort by the Emergency Peace Federation to bring sanity to the scene. The ad brought in $35,000 in an emotional outburst for peace. The AUAM mailed out 100,000 postals for a "peace or war" referendum, urging the president to let the people decide.

While the Sixty-fifth Congress was in emergency session on April 2 to hear President Wilson's war message, a delegation of fifty carrying The Hague peace flower, the white tulip, descended on Washington, making hasty visits to Congress to urge a vote against war. Prevented by police from holding a peace parade, they demonstrated before the Capitol. That evening 500 "patriots" came over from Baltimore to break up their meeting at Convention Hall. The police looked the other way. Inside Congress that day, President Wilson was met with opposition from antimilitarist senators, among them

George Norris of Nebraska, who said war "would benefit only the class of people who will be made prosperous . . . We are going into war upon the command of gold . . . I feel that we are about to put the dollar sign on the American flag." He and others, among them Senator La Follette, were booed down with shouts of "Treason!"

President Wilson delivered his war message, "With a profound sense of the solemn and even tragical character of the step I am taking and of the grave responsibilities which it involves . . . that the United States . . . will employ all its resources to bring the government of the German Empire to terms and end the war."

Six senators and fifty representatives opposed the war resolution. Among them was the only woman member of the House, Jeanette Rankin of Montana. She said, "I love my country but I cannot vote for war." An unexpected voice in opposition to the war resolution was Claude Kitchin of North Carolina, the majority leader of the House. "I know that for my vote [in opposition] I shall be not only criticised but denounced from one end of the country to the other. The whole yelping pack of defamers and revilers in the Nation will at once be set upon my heels . . . but I can leave them [my children] the name of an ancestor who, mattering not the consequences to himself, never dared hesitate to do his duty as God gave him to see it."

Standing equally brave before "defamers and revilers" were Lillian Wald and a handful of antimilitarists, isolated from the fanfare that greeted the president's declaration of war on April 6, 1917. They found themselves with new allies, as they were linked in their opposition to war to groups of radicals and staunch pacifists. For Lillian Wald this created conflicts.

Women march down Fifth Avenue in an international protest against war, August 1914

Jacob H. Schiff

An American Red Cross public health nurse making her rounds on snowshoes in rural Main

U.S. delegates to the International Congress of Women, The Hague, 1915. Jane Addams, seated in center, second from left; Alice Hamilton standing in first row, second from left; Emily Greene Balch standing, second row, first on left; Leonora O'Reilly standing, center, second row from top; Mabel Kittredge standing first on left, second row from top; Louis Lochner in top row

Jane Addams and Lillian Wald named in Lusk Report
(New York *Evening Telegram*, June 19, 1921)

Miss Wald and her nurses supported female suffrage. The banners on this vintage automobile, about 1917, read "Votes for Women"

Visiting Nurses in front of 79th Street center, 1922

Lillian Wald and the nurses who had been at Henry Street since its founding. Seated, from the left: Annie Goodrich, Jane Hitchcock, Georgia Beaver, Henrietta Van Cleft, Roberta Shatz, Lavinia Dock and Miss Wald. Standing: Adelaide Nutting, Mary Magoun Brown and Elizabeth Frank

Miss Wald with Alfred E. Smith at a 1934 fund-raising campaign dinner. To the left of Miss Wald: Mrs. James Roosevelt and Marguerite Wales, director of nursing at Henry Street. To the right: Mrs. August Belmont, Helen Hall and Mrs. Geo. B. St. George

Visiting Nurse Service of New York

House-on-the-Pond

Miss Wald at her country home
in an earlier day with nurses
Annie Goodrich and Roberta
Shatz, and an unknown friend

Lillian Wald at House-on-the-Pond with Florette, Sarah and Hermine Cohen, June 1926

In her garden

12

War

"I K N O W the whole world is suffering from the war, but I feel
it to my very toes," Lillian Wald wrote to Ysabella Waters, who
had moved to Rochester, New York. "I feel it in every fibre of my
body. Ever since I have been conscious of my part in life I have felt
consecrated to the saving of human life, to promotion of happiness
and the expansion of good will among people, and every expression
of hatred and of the dissolution of friendly relations between people
fairly paralyzes me. I presume that is one reason why the bug [a
virus] gets so little resistance."

The declaration of war created a new reality for her as if barbed
wire had been strung across her line of vision. In the feverish war
preparations, she looked out at a nation that had assumed scarred
and grotesque forms. People were being mobilized, shaped by violence, propaganda, and new legislation. They had gone to bed in
one guise and awakened the next day masked for different roles.
President Wilson himself had told the editor of the *New York
World*, "Once lead this people into war and they'll forget there ever

was such a thing as tolerance. To fight, you must be brutal and ruthless, and the spirit of ruthless brutality will enter into the very fibre of our national life, infecting Congress, the courts, the policeman on the beat, the man on the street."

Supporting this view were statesmen such as Elihu Root, a former liberal and a cabinet member, who told a cheering audience at the Union League Club in August, "There are men walking about the streets of this city tonight who ought to be taken out at sunrise tomorrow and shot for treason."

Oswald Garrison Villard gave voice for other antimilitarists when he said that the declaration of war, "came nearer to unmanning me than anything in my life. For I knew . . . that this ended the Republic as we had known it; that henceforth we Americans were to be part and parcel of world politics, rivalries, jealousies, and militarism, that hate, prejudice and passion were now enthroned in the United States . . ."

To mobilize a divided country behind the president, George Creel, a journalist with liberal connections, was called in to head a Committee on Public Information. He enlisted in his organization journalists, educators, artists, and public relations experts, including Walter Lippmann and former muckrakers Ida Tarbell and Ernest Poole. To convince the people that the war was justified, the committee engulfed the country in a massive propaganda campaign. Through posters, bulletins, tracts and flyers, through speakers sent into towns and schools, a battle was waged for people's minds. The Espionage Act of June, 1917, and the Sedition Act of May, 1918, sealed the fate of those remnants of the antiwar movement still courageous enough to be vocal. The laws made it a crime to criticize the government, the war effort, or the draft; the laws also closed the mail to antiwar propaganda. Not only by acts of Congress, but by "intelligence agencies" set up in the departments of War, Navy, State, and the Post Office, was all opposition stifled. Thousands of private individuals joined the hunt and became amateur detectives, making it their business to collect data on professionals, labor leaders, the IWW, Quakers, radical dissenters. Vigilante groups were formed in factories and neighborhoods. In the search for enemies not a single German spy was caught, but many innocent people were defamed. Teachers were fired, among them Miss Wald's friend Emily Greene Balch; others resigned in protest over the firings, such as Charles Beard, a liberal historian at Columbia University; clergymen were unfrocked.

Except for a handful of courageous individuals like Eugene Debs and Emma Goldman who maintained public opposition to war, antimilitarism was silenced. In November, 1917, when Russian revolutionaries replaced the Kerensky regime with a new form of state apparatus called socialism, the machinery was in place to whip up a Red Scare to spread further the network of intimidation.

Certain that President Wilson was not informed about the defacement of democratic ideals, Lillian Wald undertook to tell him about it. Along with twenty colleagues she signed a letter describing "evidence of the breaking down of immemorial rights and privileges. Halls have been refused for public discussion; meetings have been broken up; speakers . . . arrested and censorship exercised . . . to prevent the free discussion by American citizens of our programs and policies." In view of the sweeping repression, she urged the president to remind the American people of their obligation in this war "to uphold in every way our constitutional rights and liberties."

What could the president say to Lillian Wald? He was agreeable, and promised that he would "have the matter in mind and will act . . . at the right time in the spirit of your suggestion." Encouraged by the president's response, Miss Wald received permission from aide Joseph Tumulty to publicize the message.

While the one-sided flood of propaganda spilled down from the war machinery, Congress speedily enacted new legislation. By the end of April, 1917, less than a month after the United States declaration of war, the Conscription Act was passed to answer Europe's clamor for American soldiers. Send us your men, "let the American flag be unfurled on the fields of France . . ." was the cry of the allies.

Miss Wald did not see war in philosophic terms, as experience beyond human understanding. Nor was she bolstered by political ideology that justified one side or the other in the conflict. Victory or defeat did not interest her. She suffered from the immorality of war, its human cost. In the Henry Street neighborhood she saw the stirrings of hatred, the attack against German and Austrian immigrants who were perceived as spies because they were born in countries that had become the wartime enemies of the United States. In her community she saw fear, even among those who had simply fled their countries to avoid conscription. Miss Wald's friend Frances Kellor had spearheaded the formation of a new organization, the Committee for Immigrants in America, to protect them from attack. Henry Street intensified its indoctrination programs to make immigrants less conspicuous by blending them into American culture.

And what better way for immigrants to show their patriotism to the United States, to demonstrate their worth and devotion, than to sign up for the armed forces? Miss Wald found the young men of Henry Street ready to enlist. She herself, torn by emotional turmoil and the human suffering in the neighborhood, tried to ease their way. She turned over one of the buildings to the draft board and made Henry Street the setting for hurried weddings and farewell parties. Uniformed Henry Street nurses took part in war parades, marching with the Red Cross, always getting a big hand. Miss Wald hastened to say that her nurses carried no war standards, they "are conservers of life." Her director of nursing, Anne Goodrich, took a leave of absence to become dean of the Army School of Nursing. And Miss Wald accepted a call to Washington to help the Red Cross formulate policy. By now, an experienced lobbyist, she immediately won for nurses rank status in the army.

On the day the United States declared war, April 6, 1917, the Federal Children's Bureau launched a year-long "Save the Baby Campaign," and Miss Wald immersed herself in the work as head of the Committee on Nursing and Child Welfare for New York City. It offered a peaceful escape from the violence of war.

She was "depressed and overwhelmed by the debasement of civil liberties," she wrote to a young man. "I understand the confusion of mind but who is not confused at this time? I feel as if the world had lost its propping, and we poor mortals are but jests, and sorry jests some of us are. I find myself in two distinct lines of activity; one seizing every opportunity to draw attention to violations of democracy, the other . . . the preservation of our home defenses, namely the care of our people, the children and industrial workers."

In the "Save the Baby Campaign" she announced a program to have every child in the city under five years of age examined. Involved in the project were over 100 organizations and countless volunteers to staff health centers. For the first time, thousands of babies received medical examinations, home care, and nursing. Through lectures mothers were educated on infant health. When the year was over, 2,000 babies among the 6,000 examined were found to have physical defects ranging from diseased tonsils to tuberculosis, hernias, and organic heart defects. Miss Wald placed special emphasis on safeguarding the health of children in wartime when families were broken up, the fathers at war, and mothers drawn into factory work. She vigorously opposed the drafting of her nurses into war service, urging that district nurses remain available to take care of the home front.

Involved though she was in health work, problems nevertheless assailed her. What, for example, was the function of an antimilitarist organization such as the American Union Against Militarism in wartime?

The executive committee, meeting in emergency sessions, tried to work out a new direction. Generally it was agreed to end all publicity and to "quietly" oppose extremes of militarism and the repression of civil liberties. But the United States declaration of war brought to the surface the basic political differences in the leadership that had been muted during three years of antiwar work.

Wald, committed to maintaining friendly relations with the government, accepted the new parameters established by the United States in its restrictive legislation at the onset of the war. Eastman, a socialist and labor lawyer, was interested in testing government restraints. Thus, Eastman, along with Roger Baldwin, Norman Thomas, and the majority of the board members, voted to establish within the AUAM a "legal defense bureau." This bureau would provide conscientious objectors with legal advice and defense and would also protect the civil rights of dissenters.

Wald had urged that the bureau become an independent organization and thereby not associate the AUAM with acts of government defiance. When her plea was turned down, she offered her resignation to the AUAM. But Eastman and others convinced her to stay on.

Wald demonstrated her support for conscientious objectors in a different way. She joined Jane Addams and Norman Thomas on a delegation to the State Department to defend the right of young men to be exempt from military service on religious and ethical grounds; she held that the United States "should not coerce men's conscience in a war for freedom." When Roger Baldwin was given a year's jail sentence for being a conscientious objector, Miss Wald visited him in prison. "She was a courageous woman, diplomatic, cautious," was the way Mr. Baldwin would describe her years later.

Still, an uneasy truce existed within the AUAM. "Without knowing it, every once in a while they do something that seems to me in such poor judgement," she wrote to Jane Addams. At a later date she made it clear that her work at Henry Street was jeopardized by her continued association with the AUAM. "There are so many things that I must plead for that I [cannot] throw away any part of my reputation for good judgement." In her estimate, the AUAM was headed for a collision course with government and, she said, "we are not by habit or temperament troublemakers."

In September, 1917, another incident took place that further revealed the cleavage in the leadership. Miss Wald protested the Post Office Department's exclusion of two AUAM pamphlets, claiming that in accordance with the Espionage Act, the material had been submitted in advance to the postmaster. She clarified her position in a letter to Wilson aide Tumulty, saying that the AUAM had never done anything "to obstruct the war or embarrass the government." She even offered to withdraw the pamphlets. Charles Hallinan and other board members opposed her action. They undertook a legal suit against the Post Office Department and urged the AUAM to show "some sort of self respect." (Four months later the organization won its case in court by proving that the pamphlets in question were indeed legal.)

She sounded a call for understanding, advising her friends that Henry Street contributors were exerting pressure. Back in February, 1916, Bruno Lasker, a German intellectual and social worker who had become a Henry Street resident, warned her, "It would be difficult to work for post war goals" if she identified with activities that appeared "to hamper the government in the effective pursuit of war."

Then a long-time supporter defected. J. Horace Harding, a banker and chairman of the board of the American Railway Express, wrote that Miss Wald and the AUAM were "disloyal and bordering on treason." She explained to Mr. Harding that she did not intend to "weaken the arms of our government but she did intend to preserve and to keep public sentiment interested in preserving the fundamental rights of the citizens of our great country. . . ."

And a few days before the United States declaration of war, she received a letter from Jacob Schiff from his home in Bar Harbor, Maine, telling her that Miss Addams and Miss Smith had been over to visit and that "for the time being, we occupy somewhat different standpoints." He added, "No one can foretell what may be yet before us and what everyone may be called upon to do for our Country: and one thing I am certain of, that you, dear woman will always be found in the front rank, doing your duty, no matter what your personal views and feelings may be."

How could she explain her conflicts to Mr. Schiff? She opposed war yet she supported the government; she had to protect her social programs from the loss of supporters (such as Mr. Schiff) and from wartime destruction, yet she wanted to defend the civil rights of citizens; she was a leader of the AUAM but she opposed confrontation.

While she was away from the city, the AUAM voted to send delegates to the Chicago conference of the People's Council of America, an organization that grew out of the merger of the Emergency Peace Federation and the antiwar socialists. Both Jane Addams and Emily Greene Balch supported the new organization and planned to attend the conference, but Miss Wald objected to what she called its "impulsive radicalism." She explained in a letter to Crystal Eastman that "it does not represent the organized reflective thought of those opposed to war. . . . It would be lacking in sincerity for us not to be perfectly frank with each other."

Beset with uncertainty, Miss Wald again submitted her resignation to the AUAM. The organization was in a dilemma about once more rejecting it. Miss Eastman expressed the conflict in a letter to her on August 24, 1917. "My strong feeling at present is that, while it would be very hard indeed . . . to lose you as chairman . . . not only because of your influence with the 'powers that be,' but because of your patience, devotion, wisdom, and tact . . . we would have to accede to your wishes rather than let the AUAM give up its active opposition to war."

In September, Miss Wald's resignation was accepted. She spoke for liberals, she had explained in her first letter of resignation, and "the priceless values of maintaining our country liberated from undemocratic militarism. . . . War and militarism must be combatted in more ways than one," and she was "engaged every hour of the day, almost every moment of the hour, in trying to preserve from destruction those definite programs to which I am dedicated."

The loss of Miss Wald's leadership was a blow to the continued effectiveness of the AUAM. Others followed her lead and resigned from membership, among them Paul Kellogg and Alice Lewisohn. It had been Miss Wald's unique ability to bring together into working unity "people of diverse habits of thought and methods of work." After her departure, the AUAM was chaired by Oswald Garrison Villard. Finally, it evolved into the American Civil Liberties Union, founded by Crystal Eastman and Roger Baldwin, and the Foreign Policy Association, directed by Henry Street resident Adolf A. Berle.

Thus Miss Wald freed herself to join other reformers for what they called "social work" within the war process, accepting appointments to committees of the Council of National Defense. Grace Abbot, Pauline Goldmark, Julia Lathrop, and others found it easier to be on the fringe of the war effort than to maintain unequivocal opposition to the government. Florence Kelley became secretary of the Board of Control of Labor Standards for army clothing, doing her part for labor and the war mobilization.

Nothing would ever again be the same for Lillian Wald. Many of her closest friends had left Henry Street. Anne Goodrich was on temporary leave, Ysabella Waters had retired to Rochester, Helen McDowell was ill, and Lavinia Dock had moved to the family homestead in Fayetteville, Pennsylvania. Miss Dock had written a formal note to Miss Wald, "As it is possible, indeed certain, that I shall not return to New York to live, . . . I feel it necessary to resign as a member of the Henry Street Corporation in order that some active member may take my place . . ." Miss Dock explained that she was "not at all out of the movement, even though I am not on the committee." Despite frequent differences of opinion, the two women remained warmly devoted.

Lavinia Dock had retired only from nursing. Years before she had decided to devote her energy to the suffrage movement. Critical of Woodrow Wilson for his refusal to support the suffrage amendment, she also opposed the United States entry into the war. She had allied herself with Alice Paul, a Quaker and social reformer who had gained experience in militant suffrage organizations in England, returned to the United States, and suffused new energy into the quiescent movement. Miss Paul headed the Congressional Union, and later the National Woman's Party, which waged a militant campaign for passage of a federal amendment to the Constitution to give women the vote. While Miss Wald was entering the White House to see her friend Woodrow Wilson, Lavinia Dock was on the outside picketing, carrying signs that read: "Democracy should begin at home," and "Kaiser Wilson." More than once hoodlums broke up the suffrage lines, and "patriotic" soldiers and sailors ripped banners from women's hands. In June mass arrests of suffrage pickets began, and sixty-year-old Lavinia Dock was put in prison.

Concerned over Miss Dock's welfare and the force-feeding of those women who had gone on a hunger strike, Miss Wald asked Charles Hallinan of the Washington office of the AUAM to visit Miss Dock in jail. He reported back that the workhouse in Virginia was indeed "a medieval institution if ever there was one" but "Miss Dock is taking the regimen like a veteran." She has evidently "been there before," he reported. The arrests of suffragists did not discourage Miss Dock and indeed, the wide publicity given their cruel treatment in prison brought them renewed support.

One source of continuous joy for Miss Wald during the troubled war years was her mother's residence at Henry Street. Minnie Wald had moved in a few years before when Miss Wald's sister, Julia, long widowed, remarried and gave up her large home in Rochester. Mrs. Wald knew how to make herself useful, teaching women embroidery and telling stories to young children. People loved her. Jacob Riis, on first meeting her mother, chastised Lillian Wald for her unusual reticence about her family. "It had never occurred to me that you had a family or a mother. I thought you were just you, and always had been. But your mother is a person, too."

To ease Mrs. Wald through the hot summer months, Lillian Wald rented a house in Saugatuck, near Westport, Connecticut. Though she herself could spend little time there in the troubled summer of 1917, she managed to run up for occasional weekends. The retreat from pressure soon became a necessity and at the end of the summer she bought a house and eight surrounding acres on Campo Road about two miles from the center of town. She had a gardener land-scape the grounds, creating flower beds and stands of flowering shrubs. Nothing gave her greater pleasure than to sit on the lawn overlooking the pond, inspiring her to call her country home House-on-the-Pond.

Still, there was no escaping the merciless tensions of the war years, and the feeling of isolation at not being part of the cheering multitudes. Her friend Jane Addams expressed her loneliness in stark terms when she said, "the force of the majority was so over-whelming that it seemed not only impossible to hold one's own against it, but at moments absolutely unnatural, and one secretly yearned to participate in the 'folly of all mankind.' "

In their isolation from the war fever the women for peace bonded closer together, holding meetings in secluded homes. Women such as Jane Addams, Emily Greene Balch, Lillian Wald, Leonora O'Reilly, Florence Kelley, Anna Garlin Spencer and others met and made plans to influence proceedings at the peace table in order to inject a spirit of international good will.

It was absolutely impossible for Miss Wald to pursue a consistent course; she had resigned from the AUAM yet morally she supported the antimilitarists. In September, 1917, she gave a reception at Henry Street in honor of Jeanette Rankin, the congresswoman who had voted against the United States entry into the war. A couple of months later, in November, she addressed a Woman's Citizen's dinner called by the New York State Woman Suffrage Party, the antiwar, anti-Wilson wing of the suffrage movement with which Lavinia Dock was affiliated. And in June, 1918, she wrote to Dr. Felix Adler asking him to see Crystal Eastman "re defense of Max Eastman and the 'radical element' that is back of the president [so that they] should not be estranged . . ." Max Eastman had been imprisoned under the Espionage Act and Miss Wald had come to his defense.

She was "so overwhelmed with work and with engagements," she notified a publisher that she could not possibly undertake another book. To Vida Scudder in Boston she wrote that she was "bewildered with the number of things that have fallen upon me," that "a great many schools and colleges come to see Henry Street" as a model settlement, and that it has become an attraction. And to "Dear Sister Waters," she explained, "I sometimes do not know whether I am standing on my head or my feet, so if my letters to you are inadequate please do not blame me but blame the war!"

War or no war, she had to maintain the Visiting Nurse Service and the settlement house. And she was not spared punishment for her earlier antiwar views. "I was disciplined," she would say, "by the torture-chamber method of having the money withdrawn which enabled the nurses to care for the families of soldiers no less than the other sick." She turned to the press, and in a letter to the *New York Post*, reminded the public of the work of the Visiting Nurse Service of the Henry Street Settlement and its "staff of 170 trained and skillful nurses . . . who have an organic relationship to the community."

Jacob Schiff remained one of her stalwart benefactors, successfully getting New York Mayor Mitchell and the Board of Estimate to vote an allowance for the year 1917 of $25,000 for the Henry Street nurses. He also helped her buy the Children's Aid Society property, though he cautioned her again that such an expansion would institutionalize her work. After he provided two supervisory nurses with a Ford car he told Miss Wald, "I think the next present we shall give you will be an aeroplane, better to enable you to make your flying trips to Washington and other neighboring towns."

By mid-1918, the war was winding down, but not before a world-wide outbreak of influenza and its complication, pneumonia, started on its deadly course. Twenty million civilians and combatants would be wiped out before the disease was brought under control. Miss Wald wrote to Jacob Schiff in June, 1918, that "the wolf is scratching at our door with the enormous demand for nurses . . ." And to Sister Waters she explained, "there is a demand for 40,000 nurses and a terrible shortage at the present time."

In the first days of October, 1918, 500 cases of flu were reported to Henry Street. By the twelfth of the month, Lillian Wald was appointed chief of the Nurses Emergency Council. Within twenty-four hours, she mounted a concentrated campaign from temporary headquarters in the Red Cross building on Fifth Avenue. She put under the council's jurisdiction schools, social and nursing agencies, teachers, labor, and police, to create an effective administrative machine. Calls were issued for nurse's aides and volunteers to work in homes and hospitals, to answer phones, wash dishes, and sweep floors. Nurses were called out of retirement. "You are needed," Miss Wald wired Ysabella Waters. In front of department stores college students handed out circulars that urged people to volunteer their time and advised on health precautions. Miss Wald called for house-to-house tenement inspection; she arranged with the city to feed the sick with meat and eggs. Flu victims were supplied with fresh linens and given child care and emergency assistance. To help in the rounds, she set up a motor service of automobiles and taxis. Henry Street nurses were put on round-the-clock, eight-hour shifts, going into homes where entire families were stricken with the disease and had no one to take care of them.

Before the epidemic she had written to Mary Roget Smith, "I tried not to let anyone know how unable I was to meet the day to day obligations . . . but I did go off for a rest every other week . . ."

By October 31, one month after the flu epidemic had started, she wrote to Nina Warburg, "I have worked more hours steadily than I remember ever to have worked before. Some days there has not been one consecutive hour in twenty-four undisturbed, and many times I have been as much as twenty hours in motion. Yet I feel very well . . ."

By the time World War I came to an end, the epidemic had waned. For her public health work, Miss Wald received commendations from the city and the Board of Health. To every volunteer and organization that had aided her efforts, she sent personal thank-you letters.

Jacob Schiff had his eye on practical needs and advised Miss Wald "to make an appeal to the public [for funds] immediately after New Year's before people of New York forget the splendid services rendered by you personally and the Henry Street Settlement during the Influenza Epidemic, and in connection with the demands of the Red Cross and other war work . . ." He undertook to sign such a letter of appeal.

Generous as Mr. Schiff often was, he had his moments of thrift. Without Miss Wald's knowledge, her staff wrote to him asking that he underwrite a $325 repair for burst radiators on the porch outside the room where Miss Wald insisted on sleeping, even though she was having "serious trouble with rheumatism and we feel the matter is a serious one."

In answer Mr. Schiff advised that Miss Wald sleep in her own room and "leave the windows wide open which would be effective as far as fresh air was concerned."

Miss Wald had other things to worry about. The war's end did not bring about an end to intolerance. Raids on liberals, labor, blacks, and the foreign born continued, developing into a "Red Scare" that used as its rationale the need to prevent the Russian revolution from spreading to the shores of the United States. Through violence and intimidation, conservative and "patriotic" forces created an atmosphere of fear in which every expression of liberal or radical dissent, every labor action, was threatened with reprisal.

13

A Dangerous Character

LILLIAN Wald did not escape censure during the period of the Red Scare. She was listed with sixty-two men and women in a "Who's Who in Pacifism" drawn up by Archibald Stevenson of the Military Intelligence Bureau. The list, published in leading newspapers, had been presented to the U.S. Judiciary and purported to contain those connected with "pro-German pacifist movements prior to the entry of the United States into the war." Jane Addams led the list, which included Lillian Wald and leaders of the American Union Against Militarism, among others.

Miss Wald immediately sent a telegram to Secretary Baker of the State Department. "LIST GIVEN OUT BY WAR INTELLIGENCE BUREAU AN AMAZING AND INCOMPREHENSIBLE ACT . . . AM READY TO GIVE YOU FULL STATEMENT OF MY POSITION INCLUDING CORRESPONDENCE WITH PRESIDENT WILSON!"

A month later the Overseas Committee included her among "undesirable citizens." In a letter to her Uncle Samuel Schwarz in California, she explained that the inclusion of her name and Jane

Addams's in such a list "pricked into protest" many people who would ordinarily be silent, and as a result, "the settlement never had so much support, that is quantitatively."

Not to be outdone by the federal government, New York State spawned the Lusk Committee in January, 1919, to investigate seditious activities. This committee made its chief target the "radicalism" in settlement houses and schools. Singled out for special mention in the *New York Evening Telegram* in June, 1921, were Lillian Wald and Jane Addams. An article featuring their photographs, called them two leading women "anxious to bring about the overthrow of the government and establish in this country a soviet government on the same lines as in Russia."

Fortunately Miss Wald did not have to undertake a personal defense. This was done by a parent body, the United Neighborhood Houses, who lodged vigorous protests, engaged a lawyer, and spent time, money, and energy to prove that settlements were centers of the "highest ideals and . . . strongholds of genuine Americanism in the foreign quarters of our city . . ."

Defending Miss Wald was Jacob Schiff who wrote to her secretary, "Please say to Miss Wald that I hope the stupid action in publishing her name and many others, in a so-called 'Pacifist List' is not worrying her. If only some of those who have made so much noise during the war had done half as much as Miss Wald for the American people and their cause in the war, it would be well."

Miss Wald was "touched and pleased" by Mr. Schiff's message. She had received several telegrams and letters from staunch friends who also recognized what she had done for "the people of America."

In the midst of these attacks of postwar repression, Miss Wald was sent to France by the government to represent the Federal Children's Bureau at an International Health Conference in Cannes, France, sponsored by the International Red Cross Societies. Before her departure, in March, 1919, she welcomed Anne Goodrich back to Henry Street as director of nurses, and Roberta Shatz as associate director. And on the eve of her sailing on the *New Amsterdam* she had in hand Jacob Schiff's telegram, "God bless you and protect you."

Abroad, Lillian Wald took her place as an international figure, an authority on the advantages of public health nursing in child welfare, preventive medicine, and contagious disease. She also helped the International Red Cross draw up health measures to be established in each country.

From Cannes she traveled to Paris. This city had become the center for representatives of numerous organizations that were pressing for consideration of their interests at the peace negotiations then going on at Versailles.

From Paris she continued on to Switzerland to attend the second International Conference of Women for Peace at Zurich. There she met with old friends Jane Addams, Florence Kelley, Congresswoman Jeanette Rankin, and delegates from sixteen countries. She introduced into their program measures for world-wide health care. At the Zurich conference evolved the Women's International League for Peace and Freedom, with Jane Addams as its first chairman. The organization hoped to become a moral force in the world. In their efforts to influence the Versailles Peace Conference, members vigorously opposed the regimen of starvation being imposed on Germany, describing the hunger of babies and innocent civilians as another form of violence.

After the Zurich meeting Miss Wald returned to Paris where she was appointed an advisor to the League of Nations Child Welfare Division. She instructed Herbert Hoover, head of the American Relief Administration, on the means of bringing relief to liberated countries. In now familiar terms, she said, "use plain words, and relate to the daily human experience of simple people."

Her long letters home to the family described the mood in Europe. To Rita Wallach Morgenthau she wrote in April, 1919, "the air was full of foreboding . . . France is the gloomiest. Nobody is satisfied, everybody is critical, and the situation is grave enough to warrant much of it!" A letter to other family members was nostalgic. "Every day I am reminded of my beloveds' goodness and thoughtfulness for me. The trunk has *everything*. No one in France is so well cared for. Love to you all, dearest friends that ever were . . ."

At another time she signed a letter,

> "Lovingly
> Appreciatedly
> Devotedly
> Steadfastly
> Lillian D. Wald"

Back home on June 14, 1919, meant being surrounded by these dearest friends as they took over prosaic chores, unpacked her trunk, coddled her, and made her rest. It meant a welcoming telegram from the Schiffs: "both Mrs. Schiff and I feel the happier . . . that you are ours again when will you come to us for a little undisturbed possession of you Fondest love from us both." It also meant a welcome-home program of songs of different nationalities put on by Irene and Alice Lewisohn at the Neighborhood Playhouse.

Around the corner from Henry Street, at Grand and Pitt, a new red brick Georgian building with apple green shutters and front door housed a theater and dance facilities. There Miss Wald watched a program based on Walt Whitman's *Salut au Monde*, invoking an ageless lament:

> I see the battle-fields of the earth,
> grass grows upon them and blossoms and corn,
> I see the tracks of ancient and modern expeditions . . .

In the few months Miss Wald had been out of the country, the spirit of intolerance in the United States had turned into full-blown violence in which every democratic principle was under attack. The Red Scare continued unabated and was used to justify raids to ferret out "Russian agents" seeking to overthrow the U.S. government. Bolshevik conspiracies were seen in every labor strike for improved wages and conditions. And the media poured forth propaganda that proclaimed labor, the foreign born, socialists, anarchists, and the IWW were dire threats to the country.

In this period seventy different sedition bills had been put forward in Congress by the end of 1919. A. Mitchell Palmer, Wilson's attorney general, launched a nationwide crusade against the labor movement and radicals, real or alleged. In the name of patriotism, an IWW organizer, Frank Little, was dragged from a car and hanged from a railway trestle; 1,200 workers affiliated with the IWW in Brisbee, Arizona, were rounded up and driven across the border; Emma Goldman was arrested for "conspiracy against the draft," sentenced to two years in prison, and then deported to the country of her birth, Russia. Women at Radcliffe College were accused of radicalism for debating that "labor unions were essential to collective bargaining." On one night in January, 1920, 10,000 people were rounded up in simultaneous raids by agents of the Bureau of Investigation (later the Federal Bureau of Investigation).

The war was over but the country remained in the grip of repression. In the madness of violence and hatred, dissent was choked off. People stood aloof from public issues and forgot about federal responsibility, trade union organization, the uprising of women, and the defense of children. It was safer to be silent.

"Dockie dear," Lillian Wald wrote in August, 1919, "confidentially, my political attitude is making some of our generous friends uneasy and one of our largest givers—nearly $15,000 a year—has withdrawn because I am 'socialistically inclined.' Poor things, I am sorry for them—they are so scared. It is foolish since, after all, counting things in the large and wide, I am at least one insurance against unreasonable revolution in New York."

To Ysabella Waters, Miss Wald wrote, "I am spinning like a top ... I have hardly been stationary in one spot since my return [from Europe in June]." She was carrying on a heavy correspondence on a dozen different issues. "I am going to have a terrible struggle about money. The rich people are most panicky these days with regard to anyone who stands out for liberalism. When I see you next, I will tell you of some of the houndings."

The houndings notwithstanding, Miss Wald wrote to Sister Waters that she had launched a campaign for one million dollars, much to her despair. She had to supply funds for a staff now grown to 212 nurses who annually made over 330,000 visits to 42,000 patients.

Poor health aggravated her burden of responsibility. Despite a robust appearance she had no energy, she wrote to Jacob Schiff, repeating to him her worries about finances. But Schiff had predicted that the larger her organizations grew, the more funds she would need, and raising money now absorbed all her time. He continued to be her ally and he approached John D. Rockefeller on behalf of the million-dollar campaign for the Visiting Nurse Service which he called "a city institution of the first importance." He was pleased to receive the reply that funds would be forwarded from the Laura Spelman Rockefeller Memorial Foundation.

No contributions were more valued than those that came from former Henry Street club members. To Aaron Rabinowitz, an original member of the American Hero Club, who sent a large contribution, she wrote: "I am nearly proud to bursting over this son of mine! . . . The real happiness that wells from my heart that the boys whom I have cared for and loved so long are becoming partners in every way."

As in the war years, conditions had created new imperatives. New organizations sprang up to prevent the dismantling of welfare programs and to protect civil rights. Like Miss Wald, their members refused to be silenced by the Red Scare. At the very height of it, she fearlessly supported diplomatic relations with the Soviet Union, asking Carrie Chapman Catt to join her. "It would be of immeasurable value to have your woman's mind, experience and prestige!" she wrote. And she confounded her critics by agreeing to serve with the Women's Memorial Association for Theodore Roosevelt, a wartime hawk, at the same time that she joined a new liberal organization called the People of America Society. In these complex times, she felt some sense of victory when the Senate finally ratified the nineteenth amendment giving women country-wide the right to vote.

Bringing to a climax the turmoil of the period was the sudden death of Jacob Schiff in September, 1920. His last letters to Miss Wald forewarned of his illness, complaining of "sleeplessness," and his "nerves playing tricks." Although her strength and influence stood on their own foundations, she experienced a stab of panic, as if a tower had been tipped, when she realized that the prestigious man who had spread his mantle of friendship and support around her life's work was gone. Her words in tribute were sedate when she called attention, in an obituary for the *Survey*, to his generous support for community programs remote to his experience and interests, such as child labor amendments and improved labor conditions.

The death of her benefactor sounded the final chord, the coda to an age. A twenty-seven year relationship that had spanned the Progressive Era was brought to a close at a time when progressivism itself lay shattered by persistent attacks and raids.

A month later it was announced that Mr. Schiff's estate had bequeathed a gift of $300,000 to the Henry Street Settlement for the construction of a central administration building for the Visiting Nurse Service. The completion of the new building at 99 Park Avenue both facilitated and complicated Lillian Wald's life. Although the administration of the service was completely in the hands of Anne Goodrich, nevertheless it still required the executive direction and fund-raising powers of Lillian Wald. She found herself traveling between Park Avenue and Henry Street.

Among those not convinced that Miss Wald was a dangerous radical was President Woodrow Wilson who appointed her to the general steering committee of an Industrial Conference in Washington in October, 1919, which had been called to discuss the threat of labor strikes in the steel, coal, and railway industries. Miss Wald stated at the conference that wage earners had the right to join labor organizations of their choice and bargain collectively. And in a letter to Edward Slossen, editor of the *Independent*, she showed her insight into the attack on aliens, calling it "a kind of smokescreen to deflect the attention from the real conflict, that between capital and labor."

President Wilson, worried about the country's turn to postwar isolationism, undertook a nationwide speaking tour. He tried to arouse public pressure on Congress to ratify the League of Nations, an international organization created at the Paris Peace talks to mediate world problems. The president had staked his reputation as the architect of world peace on a new system of collective security. But Congress rebuffed him and voted against participation by the United States in the League. The combination of a taxing tour, congressional defeat, and the resurgence of physical and emotional frailties, brought on a massive stroke. For seventeen months, until the end of his term, Wilson was partially paralyzed and unable to carry on the functions of the presidency.

The 1920 presidential election brought to office an obscure Republican senator, Warren G. Harding, who, with the two succeeding Republican presidents, Calvin Coolidge and Herbert Hoover, shaped postwar conservatism. New propaganda—affluence and success were now within everyone's reach—dominated the media. "Two cars in every garage" and "a chicken in every pot" became the smart talk of the Jazz Age and the Roaring Twenties, as the decade was called. Forgotten were the unprivileged, once more made invisible.

In the changing political climate, Lillian Wald remained a national figure but no longer the national leader of prewar years when she had helped direct the country in social reforms. The postwar years required different heroes and heroines. Though she was in demand for her support and advice, there was a different tone to it, like an echo of the past.

Somewhat wistfully she wrote to Lavinia Dock complaining that no publication—almost none—recorded that she was *the first public health nurse.* A letter she sent to the New York Mission Society informed them that "our organization is original and is based upon the independence of the nurses' service. . . . We did originate the term 'Public Health Nurse.' "

In the changing times, Lillian Wald understood the need for flexibility if settlement houses were to continue. Not only was the postwar mood conservative but her own neighborhood had changed. Old immigrant families had moved to better communities and the new Lower East Side population, many of whom were black or Hispanic, had different requirements. Funds for programs were more difficult to get. Above all, she had witnessed the gradual professionalization of social work as it incorporated a new body of knowledge derived from the field of psychiatry. An individual's personal problems were considered divorced from the social fabric. No longer were social workers identified with social reform. And no longer did they choose to live among the needy. Instead of helping neighbors, caseworkers were helping clients. The change in approach struck Miss Wald when she asked a young social worker, recently graduated from college, to visit a neighborhood woman who was pregnant and unmarried. The social worker demurred, claiming she had no experience doing casework. "Who said anything about casework?" said Miss Wald. "I asked you to go and see a girl!"

The cooperation of old-time club members lifted her spirits in those dark years as they began to share with her the responsibilities of the settlement house. Many became active board members and trusted assistants.

The waning of her influence that had started with the declaration of war continued. She was fighting defensive actions, trying to hold on to progressive gains, and at the same time talking up in support of victims of intolerance. It was an act of courage, in 1922, during the Red Scare, to join a group of liberals who won the release of the Reverend John Haynes Holmes and Norman Thomas after their arrest for speaking on a street corner in Mount Vernon, New York. "Lovers of Freedom must rejoice," Miss Wald declared. "It is a hopeful sign. It may be that we are recovering from the war-time hysteria. Let us hope so."

Her fight for freedom and justice did not diminish, and she gave her distinguished name to bolster struggling new organizations. Unknown to her, the Federal Bureau of Investigation was monitoring her activities. Among the dossiers they compiled on individuals and organizations, one referred to the "radical coterie which gravitates around Lillian Wald and Florence Kelley . . ."

In 1922, she undertook the vice-presidency of the American Association for Labor Legislation. Her name appeared on the committee for the freedom of Nicola Sacco and Bartolomeo Vanzetti, two Italian laborers accused of the murder of a factory paymaster and his guard, despite testimony supporting their claims to innocence. She contributed to the American Anti-Imperialist League, dedicated to the independence of the Philippine Islands; and she sponsored the American League to Abolish Capital Punishment. She also added her name to the Tom Mooney Defense Committee. Mooney, an active labor leader, had been accused of setting off a bomb in a San Francisco Preparedness Day parade in which a participant was killed. After his imprisonment, an upsurge of protest resulted in getting his death sentence commuted to a life term. (He was freed unconditionally in 1931 when new testimony by a perjured witness was presented.)

Accompanied by Elizabeth Farrell, Miss Wald sailed for Europe in April, 1924. In England she dined at the home of author John Galsworthy and met other authors, notably H. G. Wells and Thomas Mann. Her tour took her to the Soviet Union in response to a government invitation requesting her advice on health matters. On her return home, she was criticized for traveling to a Socialist country with which the United States had no diplomatic relations, but she maintained she saw nothing wrong with giving health advice. Shrugging aside criticism, she became the vice-president of the American Society for Cultural Relations with Russia (U.S.S.R.).

A list of the organizations Miss Wald supported would trace the pattern of liberal activity during the postwar decade. With old-time reformers Jane Addams, Felix Frankfurter, Oswald Garrison Villard, Florence Kelley, author-teacher Scott Nearing, and a handful of others, she joined labor and radical coalitions to keep social activism before the public. They spoke up not only in defense of civil liberties but also mounted an attack against the racism of the Ku Klux Klan, which by 1924 claimed a membership of four million. The Klan was dedicated to cleansing the white race of taints by blacks in particular, and also by Catholics and Jews. It forced its views onto every aspect of life through threat and intimidation. Racism was particularly offensive to Miss Wald, who by 1925 had twenty-six black people on her staff, making up one-fifth of her personnel.

In those trying years there was also the pain of personal loss. In 1923 her mother died. "Dear Uncle Sam: I do feel the ache terribly as if I had lost my child . . . She [mother] had been reading the Bible a good deal and we buried her precious book with her . . ." A year later her younger brother Gus died. Of the family only Lillian and her sister, Julia, remained, and although they were devoted to each other, each had gone her own way.

By the end of 1924, she was again in the midst of raising money, this time to increase nurses' salaries. To a friend she wrote in December, "It has been a terribly hard fall for me, as you would know . . ."

Worn down by years of conflict and relentless battles against intolerance, she could no longer boast of robust health. At her physician's insistence that she must take a rest, she traveled to Mexico with Jane Addams and Mary Roget Smith in March, 1925, for a six-week trip. The women did the usual sightseeing but were also guests of President Callas. While on her travels, Miss Wald became ill and ascribed it to an attack of dysentery. On her return home, doctors made a more accurate diagnosis of her intestinal infection. She underwent surgery for a hysterectomy and appendectomy. At the end of April, Lavinia Dock wrote to her. "Dearest—I could scrape up some money if you need—you have done the same for me . . . and I am not telling anyone that you are ill in the hospital for I know you would dislike being thought just a mere mortal . . ." But word spread that Lillian Wald was ailing, bringing hundreds of get-well messages from staff, friends, neighbors, and even strangers. A note from Florence Kelley told it all. "Dearest Lady: Your triumphs are many. But all the sweetness and goodness in people that you have released and that is flowing out to you in love and gratitude and healing is the best. God Bless you. Florence."

Miss Wald's recovery brought this comment from Lavinia Dock. "Dearest . . . you do your illnesses and recoveries in the same dazzling form and with the vivacity and originality as all other deeds!"

To complete her convalescence, Miss Wald spent two weeks in a sanitarium in Battle Creek, Michigan. She returned to Henry Street in her usual "dazzling form" but in reality she would never fully regain her unbounded energy. She celebrated her return to work by inviting a party of friends including authors Edna Ferber, Willa Cather, and Fannie Hurst to see the play *The Dybbuk* at the Neighborhood Playhouse. This first English production of the famous

Yiddish play had opened to critical acclaim and Miss Wald was besieged for requests for tickets.

For ten years the Neighborhood Playhouse, under the direction of Irene Lewisohn and Alice Lewisohn, had been a showcase for experimental and innovative programs. Distinguished theater people came there to perform, among them Ethel Barrymore and Ellen Terry. The Duncan dancers, Isadora's "children," delighted audiences as did the Indian poet Rabindranath Tagore who made the pilgrimage downtown. A child who had sneaked into the theater whispered to Miss Wald when she saw the venerable poet enhanced by a full flowing beard and dust-colored robe:

"Is that God?"

"No," whispered Miss Wald, "but a friend of His."

Another source of cheer were the Henry Street clubs which had an enrollment of 1,450 youngsters for the 1925-26 season. The clubs had undertaken to provide music lessons—piano, violin, voice, and chorale. Teenagers such as Anna Sokolow, Sophie Maslow, and Edith Segal were taking lessons with Miss Irene that sparked their later careers in dance.

Toward the end of the decade, Miss Wald embarked on another million-dollar fund-raising campaign, during which she made every effort to get support from the public health department. Giving her invaluable assistance was Alfred E. Smith who, after his defeat in the 1928 presidential election, became an active member of the Henry Street board of directors. Night and day, Miss Wald was involved in social events, publicity, and every measure that would guarantee the survival of her expanded organizations.

She came home to Henry Street on the eve of her sixtieth birthday in March, 1927, to find the settlement filled with friends, former club members, and a delegation from the police and fire departments who handed her a gift of a box filled with $122.02 in pennies.

The decade was coming to a close but not without tragedies brought on by mindless intolerance. In August, 1927, she received a telegram from the Sacco and Vanzetti Defense Committee: "Have been authorized . . . to invite you to peacefully attend demonstration outside Charlestown prison night of execution. The conscience of

America will be mobilized." In 1929, Lillian Wald was still signing petitions to the president urging that he restore citizenship rights to the 1,500 men and women convicted under the Espionage Act.

In 1929 the stock market crash ushered in the worst economic depression in the history of the country.

And Lillian Wald was very tired. The permanent endowment she had hoped for never materialized and each year she had to embark on the tiring round of fundraising. The havoc brought on by the Great Depression was something she could not handle. She let it be known among friends and supporters that she was worried about the future, that "the time was coming when Henry Street will have to stand on its own feet."

14

"Where the Winds Do Blow"

EVERY spring from the windows of her Connecticut home she observed the countryside come back to life, the flush of green spreading over the background hills, and tiny buds sprouting on nearby shrubs. Over the pond dipped yellow-green sprays of the willow trees, and through patches of mud and snow crocuses pushed their way, delicate plants to withstand lingering winter frost. At last she had time to appreciate the beauty of nature, which moved her to tears, she said.

As the summer came on, she would sit outdoors near the flower beds, newly planted in 1931. "Indeed I want flowers," she wrote to the landscapist who had pruned old trees and set in new ones. "I am quite excited over the anticipated pleasure of seeing the garden this summer." When she had strength for it, friends came to call, old friends from Henry Street and Westport friends who had incorporated her into their lives. Ill health had become chronic in the early 1930s at about the same time the economy had tumbled into a world-wide depression, and a new siege of poverty lay hold to the Henry Street neighborhood.

"It was exactly like a temperature chart," she said, the way "sick children show the curve when financial depression occurs." Only in the early days of the nursing service had she seen such desperation. The problems her nurses and supervisors were forced to handle were "beyond description." The shutting down of home relief bureaus, or their temporary closure, "and the pitiful appeals of families in desperate conditions are nearly unbearable." In a report Miss Wald stated, "Starvation is serious for the adults; it is hideous for the children when we know that they will suffer all the rest of their lives because of their tragic experience." She was filled with despair that she could not raise sufficient money to feed the hungry and ailing. In spite of the crises, New York Mayor Walker denied her funds for the nursing service.

Even so, Henry Street became a haven during the depression. Children from every part of the city asked to be sent to its camps; its sixty clubs enrolled thousands; the Neighborhood Playhouse continued to train youngsters in theater arts and the dance. And the Visiting Nurse Service had grown to twenty centers, handling close to 100,000 cases a year. Miss Wald appealed to the city and state for financial aid, but not until the federal government stepped in at a later date to provide welfare was her burden lightened. By that time, she could only appreciate the changes from Connecticut.

In 1930 she put her personal affairs in order and made out a will, appointing as executors her sister, now Julia Cordley, and two Henry Street friends, Rita Wallach Morgenthau and Hyman Schroeder. In the disposal of her estate, she requested that the "brasses and coppers" and other antiques at Henry Street should remain there undisturbed, "for the things I have put there, I think, give it some of its atmosphere . . ." She divided her personal possessions and estate among family and friends.

Early warnings coming from abroad about the growing anti-Semitism in Germany alarmed her. Still, her identification as a Jew did not grow stronger. She scorned religious categories, she told an interviewer for the *New York World Telegram* in December, 1930. They "pigeon hole people," store them and forget them. "People are fed or hungry; warm or cold; well or sick; happy or unhappy." These were the only classifications she recognized.

No longer able to concentrate her inner forces into a show of strength, her activity continued in low key—occasional meetings, fundraising, and writing letters to her large following. "Of course, I remember you," she wrote to Harry Spector, "how perfectly ridiculous to think I could forget you!—Keep in touch with the settlement. I remember how much help you have been to us."

She commiserated with her Uncle Samuel Schwarz who complained about lessened vitality, "for though I am a little younger than you, I am experiencing the same indications of strain on body and mind."

She carried on and joined Jane Addams in Washington in December, 1931, for a disarmament meeting. Miss Addams had recently won the Nobel Peace Prize, sharing it with Dr. Nicholas M. Butler, head of Columbia University. That same month, both Miss Wald and Miss Addams gave a radio address at a luncheon of the Women's International League for Peace and Freedom.

Late in 1932 she again underwent surgery. To hasten her convalescence, her sister, Julia, took her to Italy. But Miss Wald could not wait to return to Henry Street and to House-on-the-Pond. By remaining in bed part of each day she managed to get around. When doctors diagnosed her ailment as a cardiac problem and chronic anemia of "mysterious origin," the course of her life underwent dramatic change.

A flu attack in 1933 further weakened her. Dire predictions were handed out by doctors and nurses. When it looked as if the end was near, the press was alerted to her condition. But she pulled out of the illness and her birthday that year became an occasion for true celebration. Cards, letters, flowers, and gifts poured in. From sister Julia, "I love you more than tongue could tell." The Henry Street family wrote, "thank God that you were born and [we] pray God that each day may bring your return to us one day nearer. Happy birthday, dear Lady, God bless you."

Too ill to attend Henry Street's fortieth anniversary celebration, she received a full report of telegrams from President and Mrs. Franklin D. Roosevelt, the Ramsay MacDonalds, Governor and Mrs. Herbert Lehman, U.S. Secretary of Labor Frances Perkins, Jane Addams and Mary Roget Smith, among hundreds of others. She in turn sent her message to "dear comrades who have built the House of which we are so proud."

Lavinia Dock, in letters to Adelaide Nutting, expressed her concern about the Lady. "I am deeply anxious about Lillian," she wrote. "Her ailments and their symptoms sound to me very serious . . . Her recuperative powers and nerve elasticity and endurance are marvellous but I do feel she will have to give up all responsibility and activity and that will break her spirit."

Indeed in 1933 Lillian Wald resigned as head worker of Henry Street and announced that Helen Hall of Philadelphia would replace her. But she continued as president of the board of directors, and although physically removed from Henry Street, she remained involved by reading reports and minutes of meetings. Her lack of self-pity changed Miss Dock's perspective. "It is almost a marvel about Lillian," she wrote to Miss Nutting. "All along her spirit and courage and even gayety have been unaltered even when she could hardly move. Now she is writing her second twenty years, full of enthusiasm, having visitors stay with her and all, but something is wrong with one knee and she can't walk without a prop—can't go up and down stairs so a little elevator was put into her house. It is a mournful thought that someone else is in her place at 265 but all agree that Helen Hall is a fine woman."

Friends would have come in a steady stream if she had not established hours for visits. Invited to tea with their families were old-time Henry Street club members Aaron Rabinowitz and Irving Cohen, American Hero Club members who had homes in Westport. One of Mr. Cohen's three daughters, Hermine, would recall in later years that she was brought up in the Lillian Wald tradition—with compassion for people and involvement in liberal causes. She remembered sharing her gifts for her seventh birthday with Henry Street children, and learning Esperanto to please Miss Wald, who had always hoped that a universal language would unite people of different lands.

Or Miss Wald would write a letter to Hyman Schroeder's nephew, Herbert Abrons (son of Anne Schroeder and Louis Abrons), a law student at Yale, to suggest that he come to Sunday dinner and bring along with him Florence Kelley, also a Yale law student and a granddaughter of Miss Wald's friend Florence Kelley. "Will you be a good boy," she wrote to Mr. Abrons, "and make a slight survey of your college and let me know what change there is in the students' views? I am aware that there is a strong antiwar or pacifist movement but I would like to know what it is." Miss Wald was well aware of the sinister signs of another war and a holocaust brewing in Germany.

There was also the Westport community of artists and writers, among them Van Wyck Brooks, who encouraged Miss Wald to write the second volume of her memoirs, called *Windows on Henry Street*. Other guests came calling. Eleanor Roosevelt rode down from Hyde Park, New York. Albert Einstein traveled over from Princeton, New Jersey; Governor and Mrs. Lehman came down from Albany; and neighbors, judges, lawyers, friends, young and old.

Jane Addams was always welcome, riding over from Hadlyme, Connecticut, where she was staying with a friend in the summer of 1934. The two women sat in the garden thinking afresh over the hard times, discussing the New Deal as fulfillment of their own work.

And Lavinia Dock maintained her vigil, listening to the whispers of the inner person: "then went to Lillian's and was there for five days. Her recovery is a marvel for she is so exactly her old self *except no reserve strength*, . . . but spirits and personality undimmed, shining like the sun on all around.

"But she is terribly anxious over the Jewish troubles and I am sure, Adelaide, that our dear, good friends among them here are really alarmed—even terrified. I am more distressed about it than I can say. Is there anything we could do? I know they say that Christians should protest more concretely and so they should—but how? . . . Lillian wrote to one of the heads of the YWCA [Young Women's Christian Association] asking if that organization could not protest on the grounds that inhumanity to one threatens all—and the general denial of Christian ethics in Nazism but I fear that the Y.W.s will have little influence on anyone."

Miss Wald had also written a letter to Mrs. John D. Rockefeller, Jr. in 1934, denouncing "the propaganda which infiltrates America's life and America's thought" as the most disastrous thing in her recollection. Such hatred, she wrote, "jeers at all the good and the spiritual that have been developed since the dawn of conscience. . . . Though Hitler anti-Semitism is more brutal than anything else they do, . . . it is fundamentally not more dangerous than other outrages; . . . than the suppression of Catholic freedom and liberal thought, and the suppression of the rights of women. But anti-Semitism is the easiest red herring to deflect people . . ."

Again, in a letter to a Sunday School class in Bath, New York, in 1936, she spoke out, putting forward her personal philosophy that there is "a brotherhood of man: that people should strive to understand each other and to give allegiance to each other; and that anti-Semitism and anti-anything-else that discriminates against human beings who meet the ethics of society really insults Jesus and His teachings."

But Lavinia Dock always had special insights into Lillian Wald. "O, Adelaide," she wrote to Miss Nutting, "I often wish she [Lillian] could pass beyond before the Jewish horror in Germany gets even worse as it will. I had a letter from someone in another place which said that Hitler intends pursuing and hounding the Jews in every country so far as he possibly can. He really wants to *exterminate* them and as he can't do that he wants to develop persecution all around the world. Much as I love Lady I would be glad to see her go. Her life is done. She must spend it in being careful of that heart—so weak and yet so strong—I am crying; you must excuse it. She never mentions the Jewish tragedy to me. She is so self-controlled and so courageous. I believe she has a nurse with her all the time now." But Lillian Wald was not ready to silence her voice.

In the 1936 presidential campaign, she publicly supported the reelection of Franklin D. Roosevelt. And although retired from Henry Street, she was again vilified, this time by a handful of anti-Roosevelt conservatives. "Some day I will relate to you all the persecutions and funny stories of the campaign," she wrote to Eleanor Roosevelt.

She had had much to mourn, such as the death of Florence Kelley in 1932, at whose memorial services she had said of her friend, "She was not afraid of truth, she was not afraid of life, she was not afraid of death, she was not afraid of enemies." And when Jane Addams died in 1935, Miss Wald herself was too ill to do more than privately mourn her passing. In 1936, her Uncle Samuel Schwarz died, an aged man of ninety-two who bequeathed to her and a nephew his entire estate.

But like the spring renewal outside her window were the healing qualities of "sweetness and goodness" that she had released in people, now flowing back to her in "love and gratitude" as Florence Kelley had pointed out years before. And while she sat quietly at home, her seventieth birthday was being triumphantly celebrated, messages pouring in from around the world. On that day, she gave up her last active post with the settlement, becoming president emeritus of the board of directors. Special articles in newspapers and magazines paid her homage for her contributions to public health and social welfare, calling her one of the great women of the century. In Congress she was praised by Representative Emanuel Celler.

On her birthdate, she tuned in to a special radio broadcast to hear herself acclaimed by President Franklin D. Roosevelt whose message was read by his mother, Mrs. James Roosevelt. Also extolling her were Governor Lehman and Mayor La Guardia, who presented her with the distinguished service certificate of the City of New York. And others—Fannie Hurst, former Judge Jonah J. Goldstein, A. A. Berle—recalled her beginnings and the founding of the nursing service.

At Henry Street itself hundreds of neighbors gathered for a special birthday party in the gymnasium where the oldest member of the settlement lighted candles on a thirty-pound birthday cake. Ready to be delivered to Miss Wald was a sterling silver tray engraved with signatures of friends and supporters. The people of Westport, too, honored their famous neighbor, presenting her with a large volume of poems, drawings, greetings and 1,200 signatures of the well known as well as everyday neighbors.

Miss Wald summed up her thoughts to a *New York Times Magazine* interviewer in March, 1937. She spoke like a stateswoman who had looked out at the world and learned at last that it was not enough only to inform the public of injustice. She had fought battles over and over again to build into the social structure of the country provisions for justice and human welfare. Commenting on the changed mental attitude of the unprivileged, she observed that they no longer viewed themselves as "the disinherited but regard themselves as endowed with the right to share in new standards of comfort and . . . dignity." She remarked particularly about the attitudes of the women of the Lower East Side who now went themselves to Albany to demand their rights instead of having others speak for them.

Social security, old age pensions, unemployment insurance, and other measures of the programs instituted by President Roosevelt and called the New Deal were only a recognition of a minimum standard of living "below which it is the duty of the government to see that no one shall fall."

She completed the interview by stating her faith in the "children of today . . . to obtain a more reasoned and more equitable society . . ." Young people show a definite comprehension of this changing world, she said. It was on them that "we must depend for organized action" to solve social problems.

Celebrations of her unique accomplishments went on while the Lady was alive to enjoy them. On Cherry Street, in the heart of the district she served, a playground was dedicated to Lillian Wald in June, 1937, "in appreciation of her pioneer work for children and district nursing in this city." Playgrounds, the Visiting Nurse Service, the Henry Street Settlement House, the Federal Children's Bureau, the school nurse—would become enduring reminders of Lillian Wald's vision and of her ability to make a reality of that vision. Through her conception of the public health nurse, she brought health care and medical knowledge to families in urban centers and in the isolated countryside. Indeed the concept of the public health nurse has spread to every corner of the world.

Never was she unmindful of the love with which she was surrounded. She wrote about it to Harry Z. Cohen, a founding member of the American Hero Club, and his family.

Very dear Anna and very dear Harry and very dear all their children:
I am out of expressions—I am counting on my credit with you and my other dear friends to feel my appreciation and my gratitude and my very dear love. There never was anybody in the world that got so much as I and the matter of not being able to walk seems a trifling thing. I would hardly notice it if I could accomplish something of what I need legs for.

This is just a preliminary letter to you for I am so rich in tokens of friendship and love that, as I said "the very heavens seem to pour it" but I don't want to wait any longer to say thank you to you dear people.

Affectionately,

(Lillian D. Wald)

To the final days, she remained alert to the dangers threatening Europe. She wrote to Governor Lehman, "Such a hectic time as we are having. I feel it in bed as much as you would feel it where the winds do blow. . . ."

In September, 1940, Lillian Wald died of a cerebral hemorrhage. She was mourned by thousands at private and public meetings. At Henry Street's Neighborhood Playhouse, the service was led by Rabbi Stephen S. Wise of the Free Synagogue. Dr. John L. Elliott of the Ethical Culture Society officiated at a private service at her Westport home. A few months later, at a Carnegie Hall Memorial meeting, 2,500 people gathered to exchange stories, to listen to messages from the president and the governor, and to hear speakers Mayor La Guardia and other friends reach into history and poetry to capture her "human goodness," as author Van Wyck Brooks expressed it. They extolled her courage and vision. They called her one of the great women of all time, and they told of her leadership in struggles that know no end.

Epilogue

Dear Miss Dock,

March 10th is Miss Lillian D. Wald's Birthday.

There will be a few spring flowers in each of our district nursing offices to commemorate this day. But more important will be the fact that our public health nurses will be carrying out Miss Wald's ideas of service to families needing skilled nursing care. We will visit in many homes to give care to the sick just as Miss Wald did on the day she founded this organization.

We have accepted the trust and faith which Miss Wald handed down to us and it is our aim to maintain for the people of New York a high standard of public health nursing service.

As one of Miss Wald's friends and admirers I wanted to send you this message on the anniversary of her birth.

Very sincerely,

(signed) Marian G. Randall,
Executive Director
VISITING NURSE SERVICE OF NEW YORK

That same "trust and faith," handed down by Lillian Wald continues to inspire surviving neighbors, friends, club members and/or their descendants; indeed, it found expression in the city of New York itself.

On October 4, 1947, the cornerstone was laid on the Lower East Side for the Lillian Wald Houses, one of the early low-income housing developments.

Governor and Mrs. Lehman, seeking to memorialize the death of their aviator son Peter, shot down in World War II, added a building called "Pete's House" to the Henry Street Settlement complex of buildings in 1948.

In 1970, Miss Wald was inducted into the Hall of Fame of New York University where she took her place as the first Jew to be elected to that body since its founding in 1900. Presented to the Hall in honor of the occasion were a bronze bust by sculptor Eleanor Platt and a medal by Malvina Hoffman. Heading the committee to promote her election was Aaron Rabinowitz, an original member of the American Hero Club.

In 1974, the American Nurses Association formed its own Hall of Fame. Among the first inductees were Miss Wald and her colleagues and friends Lavinia Lloyd Dock, Anne W. Goodrich, Mary Adelaide Nutting, and Margaret H. Sanger.

In 1975, the Louis Abrons Arts for Living Center was dedicated to provide workshop and exhibition facilities in the performing and visual arts. This center, an extension of the Henry Street Settlement House, was created by the Abrons-Schroeder descendants to memorialize their father and their own continuing commitment to the values of Lillian Wald.

Standing as perpetual reminders of their founder are two organizations made separate legal entities in 1944. The Henry Street Settlement House continues to serve the needs of the Lower East Side. The Visiting Nurse Service of New York, located on the upper East Side, is dedicated to home health care. In 1980, its field staff made over 900,000 visits in Manhattan, Queens, and the Bronx.

❧

Notes and
Sources

Abbreviations

COL   Lillian D. Wald Papers, Rare Book and Manuscript Library, Columbia University Libraries

LC   Manuscript Division, Library of Congress

NYH   Medical Archives, The New York Hospital-Cornell Medical Center

NYPL   Lillian Wald Papers, Rare Books and Manuscripts Division, The New York Public Library, Astor, Lenox, and Tilden Foundations.

TC   Nursing Archives, Special Collection, Teachers College, Columbia University

Chapter 1: THE OLD WORLD AND THE NEW

1. Ann Deborde Michael, "Jews in Cincinnati," *Cincinnati Historical Society Bulletin*, Vol. 30, 1972, pp. 152–182.
2. R. L. Duffus, *Lillian Wald, Neighbor and Crusader* (New York: Macmillan, 1938), pp. 1–15.
3. Lavinia L. Dock, in an undated letter to "Sister Taylor" about Felix Mendelssohn's oratorio *St. Paul*, mentions Rabbi Wahl's distant connection to the Mendelssohn and Wald families, Dock Papers, LC.
4. For residences and businesses of the Wald, Schwarz, and Barry families in

Rochester, see *The Rochester Directory, 1874–1914* (Rochester, New York: Drew Allis Company), Rochester Public Library.

5. Stuart E. Rosenberg, *The Jewish Community in Rochester, 1843–1925* (New York: Columbia University Press, 1954); Andrew D. Wolfe, *Views of Old Rochester and the Genesee Country: From Indian Days to 1918* (Pittsford, New York: Phoenix Press, 1970).

6. Wald to Dock, January 8, 1925, Wald Papers, Reel 2, NYPL, asks Dock on a trip to California to visit her uncle, "mother's white-haired boy took an overdose of a drug, lost his self-confidence and now owns a store."

7. Martha Cruttenden and her school, *Rochester Historical Society Publication Fund Series* (Rochester, New York, 1939), Vol. 17, pp. 157–158; Duffus, *Lillian Wald*, p. 16.

8. Walt Whitman quoted in Justin Kaplan, *Walt Whitman, A Life* (New York: Simon and Schuster, 1980), p. 233.

Chapter 2: A NEW WOMAN

1. Philip S. Foner, *Mark Twain: Social Critic* (New York: International Publishers, 1958), pp. 69–86.

2. Eleanor Flexner, "The Reform Era and Woman's Rights," in *Century of Struggle* (New York: Atheneum, 1974), pp. 203–215.

3. Emma Goldman, *Living My Life* (New York: DaCapo Press, 1970), Vol. I, pp. 16–23.

4. For a view of Rochester at that time, see *Rochester and Monroe County* (Rochester, New York: American Guide Series, 1937), pp. 65–68.

5. Application to New York Hospital School of Nursing in NYH.

6. Thorne Mansion and early training from "A Pictorial and Documentary History 1877–1979," *Cornell University Medical College Alumni Quarterly*, Vol. 42, No. 4, pp. 10–17, NYH; Helene Jamieson Jordan, *Cornell University-New York Hospital School of Nursing, 1877–1952* (New York: The Society of New York Hospital, 1952), pp. 29–31, 41–42.

7. Mary Maud Brewster's ancestry in Census for Montrose Borough, Montrose, Pennsylvania, Susquehanna County, Schomburg Center, New York Public Library; Nursing School applications of Miss Brewster and Miss Warburton in NYH.

8. Lavinia L. Dock in collaboration with Isabel Maitland Stewart, *A Short History of Nursing, From The Earliest Times To The Present Day* (New York: G. P. Putnam's Sons, 1920), pp. 117 ff.

Chapter 3: A WEEPING CHILD

1. Thirty-ninth Annual Report of the New York Juvenile Asylum, *New York Times*, February 11, 1891, 8:1; a report of a guard's cruelty to a young boy, *New York Times*, May 17, 1891, 3:3.

2. Lillian D. Wald listed in medical class, session of 1892, New York Infirmary Archives.

3. For Elizabeth Blackwell, see Flexner, *Century of Struggle*, pp. 115–119; on friendship with Florence Nightingale, p. 116.

4. Address on the Medical Education of Women at New York Infirmary Meeting, December 19, 1863, New York Infirmary Archives.

5. Lillian D. Wald, *House on Henry Street* (New York: Henry Holt, 1915), pp. 4–8.

6. According to Cyrus Adler, *Jacob H. Schiff, His Life and Letters* (New York: Doubleday Doran, 1928), p. 382, Mr. Schiff met Miss Wald through Mrs. Minnie D. Louis; Duffus, *Lillian Wald*, p. 36, says they met through Mrs. Solomon Loeb. Quoting Nina Loeb Warburg in Rita Wallach Morgenthau radio talk October 15, 1953, Wald Papers, Reel 1, Box 1, NYPL.

7. Roy Lubove, *The Progressives and the Slums, 1891–1917* (Pittsburgh: Greenwood, 1913), pp. 92 ff.

8. Wald, *House on Henry Street*, p. 9; Lillian Wald's recollections in James K. Paulding, *Charles B. Stover, 1861–1929* (New York: The International Press, 1938), pp. 131–132.

9. On settlements, see Allen F. Davis, *Spearheads for Reform: The Social Settlements and the Progressive Movement, 1890–1914* (New York: Oxford University Press, 1967), pp. 8 ff; Arthur C. Holden, *The Settlement Idea, A Vision of Social Justice* (New York: Macmillan, 1922); "A Woman's Toynbee Hall," *Review of Reviews*, July, 1890, 2:46; Vida D. Scudder, "College Settlements and College Women," *Outlook,* 70, April 19, 1902, pp. 973–976. Eighty applicants for College Settlement in Davis, *Spearheads for Reform,* p. 11.

Chapter 4: THE LOWER EAST SIDE

1. Lillian D. Wald, "The Henry Street (The Nurses) Settlement, New York," *Charities and the Commons,* Vol. 16, No. 1, April 7, 1906, pp. 1–16; Lillian Wald, *The American Hebrew,* Vol. 118, May 7, 1926, pp. 876–907; Wald Papers. Wald on district nursing, Wald Papers, Reel 24, Box 34, NYPL.

2. Wald letters to Jacob Schiff, Wald Papers, Reel 1, Box 1–2, NYPL.

3. Duffus, *Lillian Wald,* pp. 37–38.

4. Lavinia L. Dock, *The Nurses Settlement in New York,* File I, Drawer I, p. 4, TC; Wald, *House on Henry Street,* p. 12; also pp. 26–43.

5. Ysabella Waters, "The Rise, Progress and Extent of Visiting Nursing in the U.S.," *Charities and the Commons,* Vol. 15, No. 1, April 7, 1906, TC; Wald, *House on Henry Street,* pp. 53–54.

6. Wald, *House on Henry Street,* p. 33; also p. 46.

7. Moses Rischin, "The Lower East Side," in *American Vistas,* (New York: Oxford University Press, 1971), Vol. 2, pp. 44 ff; Rischin, *The Promised City, New York's Jews, 1870–1914* (Cambridge: Harvard University Press, 1962); Milton Meltzer, *Taking Root: Jewish Immigrants in America* (New York: Dell, 1976); Jacob Riis, *How the Other Half Lives*

(New York: Hill and Wang, 1957), see Preface; Hutchins Hapgood, *The Spirit of the Ghetto,* Moses Rischin, ed. (Cambridge: Harvard University Press, 1967), see Rischin's Introduction.

8. Hutchins Hapgood, *A Victorian in the Modern World* (New York: Harcourt Brace, 1939), pp. 140–143; Lincoln Steffens, *The Autobiography of Lincoln Steffens* (New York: Harcourt Brace, 1931), pp. 208–214.

9. Wald, *House on Henry Street,* pp. 13–17; Wald to Schiff, February 11, 1895, Wald Papers, Reel 1, Box 1–2, NYPL.

10. Schiff to Brewster, November 27, 1894, Cyrus Adler, *Jacob Schiff,* pp. 383–384.

11. Gutman Schwarz obituary, Rochester *Union and Advertiser,* April 15, 1892, 5:2; "Rev. Max Landsberg will officiate."

12. On Henry Schwarz, Rochester *Union and Advertiser,* August 30, 1893, 5:3; Rochester *Daily Union Advertiser,* May 7, 1894, 6:4; June 14, 1894, 6:2; May 1, 1893, 5:1.

13. Wald on Lowell, Wald to Stewart, October 10, 1910, Wald Papers, Reel 1, Box 2, NYPL. Flexner, *Century of Struggle,* pp. 206–207.

14. Louis Filler, *Crusaders for American Liberalism: The Story of the Muckrakers* (New York: Collier Books, 1961), pp. 78–79; Gregory Weinstein, *The Ardent Eighties: Reminiscences of an Interesting Decade* (New York: The International Press, 1928), Foreword by Lillian D. Wald, p. 111.

15. Duffus, *Lillian Wald,* p. 57.

Chapter 5: THE HOUSE SHE LIVED IN

1. "The Trained Nurses Settlement," *Outlook,* May 11, 1895, p. 787. Bruno Lasker, Oral History, COL, pp. 169 ff.; Dock, *The Nurses Settlement in New York,* File I, Drawer I, p. 4, TC.

2. Mary M. Roberts, "Lavinia Lloyd Dock—Nurse, Feminist, Internationalist," *American Journal of Nursing,* Vol. 56, January–June, 1956, pp. 176–179; I. M. Stewart, Oral History, COL, pp. 140, 143–146; Dock did a great deal of Wald's writing for her, p. 286; Teresa E. Christy, *Cornerstone for Nursing Education* (New York: Teachers College, Columbia University, 1969), p. 50; Lavinia Lloyd Dock parades up Fifth Avenue with Lillian D. Wald and Adelaide Nutting in suffrage parades, little "Dockie" carried the flag.

3. On Seth Low's defeat, Dock to Wald from aboard the S.S. *Potsdam,* 1903; from Florence, Italy, December 26, 1903, Correspondence, COL.

4. Georgia Beaver Judson interview, Bridgeport, Connecticut *Sunday Post,* June 4, 1939.

5. Dock, *The Nurses Settlement in New York,* TC, p. 30; Wald, "The Henry Street (the Nurses) Settlement," in *Charities,* Vol. 16, No. 1, April 7, 1906, pp. 35 ff.

6. Christopher Lasch, "Jane Addams: The College Woman and the Family

Claim," in *The New Radicalism in America 1889–1903* (New York: Vintage Books, 1965), pp. 3–37; Staughton Lynd, "Jane Addams and the Radical Impulse," *Commentary,* 32, July 1961, p. 54.

7. Ellen Condliffe Lagemann, *A Generation of Women: Education in the Lives of Progressive Reformers* (Cambridge: Harvard University Press, 1979), pp. 59–86; Allan Edward Reznick, "Lillian D. Wald: The Years at Henry Street," (Ph.D. dissertation, University of Wisconsin, 1973), describes the "Ladies of Henry Street," Chapter 4, pp. 108 ff.

8. Blanche Wiesen Cook, *Women and Support Networks* (New York: Out and Out Books, 1979). Cook, "Lillian Wald, Crystal Eastman, Emma Goldman," *Chrysalis,* No. 3, pp. 44–57; Carroll Smith-Rosenberg, "The Female World of Love and Ritual: Relations between Women in 19th Century America," *Signs,* Autumn 1975, pp. 1–29. For further discussion, see Rosalind Rosenberg, "In Search of Woman's Nature, 1850–1920," *Feminist Studies,* Vol. 3, No. 1/2, Fall 1975, pp. 141–154; Gerda Lerner, *The Majority Finds Its Past* (New York: Oxford University Press, 1979).

9. Josephine Goldmark, *Impatient Crusader: Florence Kelley's Life Story* (Urbana: University of Illinois Press, 1953), pp. 66–73; Dorothy Rose Blumberg, *Florence Kelley: The Making of a Social Pioneer* (New York: Augustus M. Kelley, 1966).

10. Rita Wallach Morgenthau, radio talk, October 15, 1953, Wald Papers, Reel 1, Box 1, NYPL.

Chapter 6: ENDANGERED CHILDREN

1. Wald, *House on Henry Street,* Chapter IV, "Children and Play," pp. 66–96; Wald to Schiff, Wald Papers, Reel 1, Box 1–2, NYPL.

2. Florence Kelley, "The Settlements: Their Lost Opportunity," *Charities and the Commons,* Vol. 16, No. 1, April 7, 1906, p. 79.

3. Guttman article, *New York Times,* March 6, 1969, 43:2.

4. The school nurse, Wald, *House on Henry Street,* pp. 51–53.

5. Opposes shorter school day, *New York Times,* April 8, 1905, 7:3.

6. "Nurses and Pure Milk," *New York Times,* February 4, 1911, 9:2, memorandum on "Underfed School Children" in Wald letter to Edgerton L. Winthrop, Jr., Wald Papers, Reel 1, Box 2, NYPL.; Wald, "Put Responsibility on the Right Shoulders," the *Survey,* November 26, 1910, pp. 315–316.

7. Child labor, Wald, *House on Henry Street,* pp. 135–151; sweatshops, pp. 153–156; tenement industry, Wald Papers, Reel 24, Box 34, NYPL.

8. Florence Kelley Wischnewetzky (her married name), "Our Toiling Children," *Our Day,* 6, September 1890, pp. 192–197; Allen F. Davis, *Spearheads for Reform,* p. 124.

9. National Child Labor Committee, *New York Times,* February 15, 1904, 14:5; June 4, 1904, 10:3; Walter Trattner, *Crusade for the Children* (Chicago: Quadrangle Books, 1970), pp. 58 ff.

10. Philip S. Foner, *Women and the American Labor Movement: From*

Colonial Times to the Eve of World War I, (New York: Free Press, 1979), Vol. 1, pp. 283–289.

11. "Mother Jones" crusade, *New York Times,* July 24, 1903, 5:5; July 27, 1903, 10:4; Elizabeth Gurley Flynn, *The Rebel Girl* (New York: International Publishers, 1973), p. 89.

12. Children's Bureau, Wald Papers, Box 34, Reel 24, NYPL. First Conference on Care of Dependent Children, 1909, *New York Times,* January 26, 1909, 10:3; Katherine F. Lenroot, "Lillian D. Wald," *The Child,* Vol. 5, No. 3, pp. 63–65; Davis, *Spearheads for Reform,* pp. 132–133; p. 123 Davis claims fight against child labor was led by reformers.

13. Wald in Washington on Children's Bureau, *New York Times,* February 4, 1909, 8:4.

14. Wald to Schiff on Children's Bureau, December 19, 1910, Wald Papers, COL; Addams to Wald, December 21, 1914, Wald Papers, Reel 8, NYPL.

Chapter 7: "WOMEN NO LONGER SPIN AND WEAVE . . ."

1. Wald, *House on Henry Street,* Chapter XI, "Youth and Trade Unions," pp. 202–215; Minnie, p. 204.

2. Morris Rosenfeld, *Songs of Labor and Other Poems,* trans. from the Yiddish by Rose Pastor Stokes and Helena Frank (Boston: Richard G. Badger, 1914).

3. Duffus, *Lillian Wald,* p. 75; statistics, p. 71.

4. Working conditions for women, see Alice Kessler-Harris, "Where are the Organized Women Workers?" *Feminist Studies,* Vol. 3, No. 1/2, 1975, pp. 92–106; "The Red Light District," Wald Papers, Reel 1, Box 2, NYPL.

5. On Leonora O'Reilly, see Meredith Tax, *The Rising of the Women* (New York: Monthly Review Press, 1980), pp. 97–100; Lagemann, *A Generation of Women,* pp. 89–112; Foner, *Women and the American Labor Movement,* pp. 294–295.

6. *New York Times,* May 12, 1902, 5:3; May 14, 1902, 6:3; May 16, 1902, 1:1; "Fierce Meat Riot on Lower East Side," May 19, 1902.

7. On Women's Trade Union League, see Nancy Schrom Dye, "Creating a Feminist Alliance: Sisterhood and Class Conflict in the New York Women's Trade Union League, 1903–1914," *Feminist Studies,* Vol. 2, No. 2/3, 1975, pp. 24–38; Helen Marot, *American Labor Unions* (New York: Henry Holt, 1914), pp. 5–10; Flexner, *Century of Struggle,* pp. 201–202.

8. *William English Walling, A Symposium,* Anna Strunsky Walling, ed. (Pennsylvania: Telegraph Press, 1938), pp. 4–8.

9. Foner, *Women and the American Labor Movement,* p. 293; Goldman, *Living My Life,* pp. 158–160; Wald, *House on Henry Street,* p. 282.

10. Wald, "Organization Among Working Women," *Annals of the American Academy of Political and Social Science,* 27, p. 638.

11. Clara Lemlich and Shirtwaist Makers' Strike, Foner, *Women and the*

American Labor Movement, pp. 326–345; Flexner, *Century of Struggle,* p. 241; Tax, *The Rising of the Women,* pp. 207–240, calls it "The Uprising of the Thirty Thousand," others call it Twenty Thousand; see "Panorama of Progress—8 ILGWU Decades," ILGWU newspaper, *Justice,* June 1980, p. 2, Archives, International Ladies Garment Workers, Union.

12. For Rose Schneiderman see Robin Miller Jacoby, "The Women's Trade Union League and American Feminism," *Feminist Studies,* Vol. 3, No. 1/2, Fall 1975, p. 136; *New York Times,* December 20, 1909, 1:2; Mrs. Belmont paid bail, *New York Times,* December 20, 1909, p. 2.

13. Wald, Tarbell, and Simkhovitch in Flexner, *Century of Struggle,* p. 243.

14. Wald talk at Dr. Stimson's church, Wald Papers, Reel 24, Box 34, NYPL; Wald, *House on Henry Street,* pp. 293–310.

15. Triangle Fire, Wald, *House on Henry Street,* pp. 208–212; Foner, *Women and the American Labor Movement,* pp. 358–361; Tax, *The Rising of the Women,* pp. 234–235; Reznick dissertation, p. 290.

16. On Lawrence Strike, see William Cahn, *Lawrence 1912, the Bread and Roses Strike* (New York: Pilgrim Press, 1980); Madeline Gray, *Margaret Sanger: A Biography of the Champion of Birth Control* (New York: Richard March, 1979), pp. 48 ff, quotes Sanger; Flynn, *Rebel Girl,* p. 142.

17. Wald, *House on Henry Street,* pp. 278–279; Addams to Wald, March 6, 1912, Wald Papers, COL.

Chapter 8: THE SUN SHINES ON EVERYONE

1. Henry Street clubs, Wald, *House on Henry Street,* pp. 179–184.

2. Herbert H. Lehman, Oral History, COL, p. 148; on formation of the Patriots Club, p. 187.

3. Morris Golden to Siegel, July 1981. Mr. Golden, founder of the Henry Oldtimers in 1938, calls himself "the oldest survivor of the nurses settlement . . ."

4. Harwood-Siegel interview, July 25, 1981.

5. Schoenfein-Siegel interview, June 23, 1981.

6. Abrons-Siegel interview, July 7, 1981; Louis W. Abrons, *My Life* (New York: Shengold, 1977).

7. Morris R. Cohen, *A Dreamer's Journey* (Boston: Beacon Press, 1949), p. 129.

8. Sobel to Wald, November 5, 1901; August 31, 1902, Wald Papers, COL.

9. Shufro to Wald, December 15, 1902, Wald Papers, COL.

10. Lagemann, *A Generation of Women,* p. 80.

11. Alice Lewisohn Crowley, *The Neighborhood Playhouse* (New York: Theatre Arts Books, 1959), pp. 4–9.

12. Lewisohn to Wald, n.d., Wald Papers, Box 14, COL.

13. Nina Loeb Warburg letters, Wald Papers, Box 14, COL.

14. "Miss Wallop," Alice Lewisohn Crowley, unpublished manuscript, *Growing Into Theatre, the Story of the Neighborhood Playhouse,* 1941.
15. Wald to Morgenthau, Louis Goodkind Collection; Morgenthau letters to Wald, Wald Papers, Box 14, COL.
16. Kittredge letters to Wald, Wald Papers, Box 14, COL.
17. Kellor to Wald, Wald Papers, Box 14, COL; Tarbell to Wald, n.d. Misc. Correspondence, Wald Papers, COL.
18. Dock to Wald, September 24, 1904, Wald Papers, COL.
19. Waters to Wald, n.d., Wald Papers, Box 15, COL.
20. Nutting to Wald, letters 1911–1914, File 2, Drawer 3, TC.

Chapter 9: THE LADY AND THE PHILANTHROPIST

1. Riis to Wald, February 12, 1904, Wald Papers, COL.
2. See Schiff letters to Wald in Wald Papers, COL.
3. . . . advised by Mr. Schiff . . . Bruno Lasker, quotes Jacob Schiff, Oral History, COL, pp. 186 ff; Dock to Wald, September 24, 1904, Wald Papers, COL.
4. On assimilation, Reznick dissertation, pp. 196–216; Irving Howe, *World of Our Fathers* (New York: Harcourt Brace, 1976), pp. 229–235.
5. "Our waste of human beings," Wald interview, *New York Times,* November 16, 1913, V, 6:1.
6. Wald to Peters, February 13, 1918, Wald Papers, Reel 1, Box 2, NYPL.
7. Adler, *Jacob Schiff,* pp. 44–50, opposed to "sort of subtle proselytizing with settlement work on East Side."
8. Jacob A. Riis House, Schiff to Wald, September 1903, Wald Papers, COL.
9. Christmas decorations, Schiff to Wald, December 22, 1914, Wald Papers, COL.
10. "Just and orderly change," Schiff to Wald, June 12, 1907, Adler, *Jacob Schiff,* p. 289.
11. Incorporation, Schiff to Wald, June 1902, Adler, *Jacob Schiff,* p. 384.
12. Male residents, Schiff to Wald, November 4, 1906, Wald Papers, COL; Wald, *House on Henry Street,* p. 58.
13. On going to Russia, Schiff to Wald, November 15, 1905, Wald Papers, COL; on mortgaging property, Schiff to Wald, January 12, 1906, Wald Papers, COL.
14. Mary White Ovington, *How the National Association for the Advancement of Colored People Began* (New York: National Association for the Advancement of Colored People, 1914).
15. Mother's accident, Wald to Schiff, September 1907, Wald Papers, COL; Kelley to Wald, September 11, 1907, Wald Papers, COL.
16. Rural nursing and the American Red Cross, Wald Papers, Reel 1, Box 2, NYPL; Lavinia Lloyd Dock, *History of American Red Cross Nursing* (New York: Macmillan, 1922), p. 212; Dock says Lillian Wald gave assistance to the New York auxiliary of the American Red Cross during the Spanish-American War (1898) but expressed dissatisfaction

even then that the organization was limited only to war and calamity; Lillian Wald, *The Red Cross Courier,* May 20, 1922, p. 4; and July 28, 1923, p. 10.

17. Metropolitan Life Insurance Company, Wald, *House on Henry Street,* p. 109; Carl Carmer, "Tower of Strength," 1959 publication of the Metropolitan Life Insurance Company.

18. Jenkins gift, Wald to Mrs. James Loeb, January 6, 1910, Wald Papers, Reel 1, Box 1, NYPL; *New York Times,* December 3, 1909, pp. 3–4.

19. Kelley to Wald, January 11, 1909, Misc. Correspondence, Wald Papers, COL.

20. Catt to Wald, 1909, Wald Papers, Reel 8, NYPL.

21. No necessity for New Year accounts, Schiff to Wald, January 5, 1909, Wald Papers, COL.

22. Trip to Japan, Schiff to Wald, Wald Papers, COL; Schiff letters, 1909, 1910; *New York Times,* July 10, 1910, V, p. 11.

23. Wald to Morgenthau, December 9, 1910, Goodkind Collection.

24. Kittredge to Wald, n.d., Wald Papers, COL.

25. Waters to Wald, August 8, 1911, Wald Papers, Box 15, COL.

26. Get-well letters, Wald Papers, Reel 8, NYPL.

27. Wald to Schiff, August 12, 1912, Wald Papers, COL; Wald to Harriman, August 10, 1912, Wald Papers, COL.

28. Wald to Schiff, November 25, 1912, Wald Papers, COL.

Chapter 10: STREET PAGEANT

1. Mt. Holyoke College at 75th Anniversary, October 9, 1912, Wald Papers, Reel 8, NYPL.

2. Columbia lecture, Wald Papers, Reel 24, Box 34, NYPL.

3. *New York Times,* June 8, 1913, II, 7:1; Duffus, *Lillian Wald,* p. 71.

4. Maggie Lynch, Wald, *Windows on Henry Street* (Boston: Little Brown, 1934), pp. 114–115.

5. Arnsteins, *New York Times,* December 5, 1913, 8:1.

6. Schiff to Wald, April 3, 1911; Wald to Schiff, November 25, 1912, Wald Papers, COL.

7. The pageant, Crowley, *The Neighborhood Playhouse,* pp. 13–15; George W. Alger, Oral History, COL, pp. 248–274; A. A. Berle, Oral History, COL, pp. 151–157; *New York Times,* June 8, II, 7:1.

8. Carole Klein, *Aline* (New York: Harper Row, 1979), pp. 57–60; Wald, *House on Henry Street,* pp. 214–215.

9. Schiff to Wald, June 9, 1913, Wald Papers, COL.

10. Wald to Morgenthau, June 1, 1913, and March 14, 1914, Goodkind Collection.

11. Walter Millis, *Road to War, America 1914–1917* (New York: Houghton Mifflin, 1935), pp. 26–32; William L. McPherson, *A Short History of the Great War* (New York: G. P. Putnam's Sons, 1920), pp. 19–30.

Chapter 11: MARCHING FOR PEACE

1. Peace material in Wald Papers, Box 88, COL.
2. Deaver to Wald, Wald Papers, Box 88, COL; Peace Parade, *New York Herald,* August 30, 1914, p. 1; Wald, *Windows on Henry Street,* pp. 286–287; the *Survey,* Vol. 32, No. 23, September 5, 1914, says there were 1,500 in the parade.
3. *New York Herald* headlines, August 30, 1914.
4. Mercedes M. Randall, *Improper Bostonian, Emily Greene Balch* (New York: Twayne, 1964), pp. 135–136.
5. Boys Clubs, *New York Times,* June 28, 1914, V, 10:1.
6. Universal Brotherhood, brochure, *Lillian Wald of Henry Street,* last page.
7. "War is a demon . . .," Alberta Eisman, *Rebels and Reformers* (New York: Doubleday, 1976), pp. 121–122.
8. Schiff on peace, feature article, *New York Times,* November 22, 1914, V, 4:1.
9. Blanche Wiesen Cook, "Woodrow Wilson and the Anti-Militarists, 1914–1917" (Ph.D. dissertation, Johns Hopkins University, 1970), pp. 6 ff; Randall, *Improper Bostonian,* p. 136; the *Survey,* March 6, 1915, "Toward the Peace That Shall Last."
10. Wald to Crandall, November 6, 1914, Wald Correspondence, 1914, TC.
11. Woman's Peace Party, Randall, *Improper Bostonian,* pp. 138–140; *New York Times,* February 5, 1915, 6:3; Ruth Pinchot, *New York Times,* February 20, 1915, 6:4.
12. Hague conference, Wald to Addams, March 25, 1915, Wald Papers, Reel 1, Box 2, NYPL; Addams in *New York Times,* May 2, 1915, V. 3; Randall, *Improper Bostonian,* pp. 132 ff; "Women's Conference Sadly Crippled," *New York Times,* April 26, 1915, 2:8.
13. On *Lusitania,* see Arthur S. Link, *Woodrow Wilson and the Progressive Era* (New York: Harper Torchbooks, 1963), pp. 164–167.
14. Liberty Festival, *New York Times,* July 5, 1915, 14:1.
15. War preparedness, Cook dissertation, p. 62; Walter Millis, *Road to War,* pp. 254 ff.
16. "Is it the duty of women to prepare for war," the *Evening Sun,* August 10, 1915, p. 6.
17. Flag Day parade, Cook dissertation, p. 55; Wald has faith in Wilson, Cook, p. 192.
18. Ford Peace Ship, Randall, *Improper Bostonian,* pp. 206 ff; O'Reilly attends, Tax, *The Rising of the Women,* p. 123; Millis, *Road to War,* pp. 243–245.
19. Wald at the Schiffs, *New York Times,* January 12, 1916, 6:4; at the Free Synagogue, *New York Times,* March 8, 1916, 18:2.
20. Attack on preparedness, Villard, in David M. Kennedy, *Over Here, The First World War and American Society* (New York: Oxford University Press, 1980), p. 32; *New York Post,* February 9, 1916, pp. 1, 2; *New*

York Times, February 9, 1916, 2:3; Wald, *Windows on Henry Street,* p. 302; on Tumulty, Cook dissertation, p. 62.

21. "Seeing Red," Wald Papers, Box 88, COL.
22. Carrizal incident, Wald, *Windows on Henry Street,* pp. 290–298; Link, *Woodrow Wilson,* pp. 141–142; Randall, *Improper Bostonian,* p. 224.
23. 1916 elections, Millis, *Road to War,* pp. 316–321; Link, *Woodrow Wilson,* pp. 247–251; Wald, *Windows on Henry Street,* pp. 299–304; on Wilson, p. 299; Cook dissertation, p. 81.
24. Wald to Hallinan, November 25, 1916, Wald Papers, Box 88, COL.
25. Warbasse quoted in Cook dissertation, p. 190; Emergency Peace Federation, Cook dissertation, p. 182; Randall, *Improper Bostonian,* pp. 227 ff.
26. Wilson attack on aliens, Kennedy, *Over Here,* p. 24.
27. Defections, Randall, *Improper Bostonian,* pp. 225–227.
28. Wald made suggestion for referendum at meeting of American Peace Society, February, 1917, at Hotel Biltmore, Wald Papers, Box 88, COL.
29. H. C. Peterson and G. C. Fite, *Opponents of War, 1917–1918* (Madison: University of Wisconsin Press, 1957), pp. 3 ff; Kennedy, *Over Here,* p. 21; Millis, *Road to War,* pp. 455–460.

Chapter 12: WAR

1. Wald to Waters, Duffus, *Lillian Wald,* p. 195.
2. Wilson to Cobb, the *New York World,* quoted in Richard Hofstadter, William Miller, Daniel Aaron, *The American Republic* (Englewood Cliffs, New Jersey: Prentice-Hall, 1959), p. 411.
3. Barbara Habenstreit, *Men Against War* (New York: Doubleday, 1970), p. 95; war hysteria, pp. 97–110.
4. Wald to Wilson, Wald, *Windows on Henry Street,* pp. 308–310; also in Wald Papers, Box 88, COL.
5. Charles A. and Mary R. Beard, *The Rise of American Civilization,* Rev. ed. (New York: Macmillan, 1956), pp. 639–650; "Let the American flag be unfurled. . . .", p. 646; Henry Street during the war, Wald, *Windows on Henry Street,* pp. 305–314.
6. "Depressed and overwhelmed . . .," Duffus, *Lillian Wald,* p. 195.
7. "Save the Baby Campaign" material, Wald Papers, Box 39, COL.
8. American Union Against Militarism minutes and material, Wald Papers, Box 88, COL, includes letter of resignation, Civil Liberties Bureau; Cook dissertation, pp. 201 ff.; *New York Times,* May 23, 1918, 2:2.
9. ". . . not troublemakers," Kennedy, *Over Here,* p. 35.
10. Wald to Harding, April 8, 1917, Wald Papers, Reel 2, NYPL.
11. Schiff to Wald, April 1, 1917, Wald Papers, COL; Wald, *Windows on Henry Street,* pp. 310–312.
12. People's Council, Randall, *Improper Bostonian,* p. 220; Cook dissertation, p. 222; AUAM minutes, June 4, 1917, Wald Papers, Box 88, COL.
13. Eastman to Wald, August 24, 1917; Wald to Eastman, August 27, 1917, Wald Papers, Box 88, COL.

14. Baldwin-Siegel interview, June 15, 1981.
15. Dock resignation, March 10, 1916, Wald Papers, Box 14, COL.
16. On Alice Paul, see Aileen S. Kraditor, *The Ideas of the Woman Suffrage Movement, 1890–1920* (New York: Anchor Books, 1971), pp. 192–194.
17. Hallinan to Wald, September 1, 1917, Wald Papers, Box 88, COL.
18. Riis quoted in Duffus, *Lillian Wald*, p. 5.
19. Randall, *Improper Bostonian*, pp. 236 ff; Jane Addams, *Peace and Bread in Time of War* (New York: Macmillan, 1922), p. 140; James Weber Linn, *Jane Addams, A Biography* (New York: Appleton Century, 1935), pp. 330–332.
20. Wald to Adler, June 19, 1918; to George B. Putnam, February 5, 1918; to Scudder, February 7, 1918; to Waters, April 1, 1918, Wald Papers, Reel 2, Box 3, NYPL.
21. Wald to the *New York Post,* June 11, 1918, Wald Papers, Reel 2, Box 3, NYPL.
22. Schiff to Mayor Mitchell and Schiff to Wald, October 22, 1917, Adler, *Jacob Schiff,* pp. 385–386.
23. Lillian D. Wald, "Influenza, When the City is a Great Field Hospital," the *Survey,* February 14, 1920, pp. 579–581; Wald, *Windows on Henry Street,* pp. 96–100.
24. Wald to Mary Roget Smith, Wald Papers, Box 39, COL.
25. Wald to Waters; Wald to Warburg, October 31, 1918, Wald Papers, Reel 2, Box 3, NYPL.
26. Schiff re sleeping porch, November 7, 1918, Wald Papers, COL; Schiff to Wald, November 6, 1918, Wald Papers, Schiff letters, COL.

Chapter 13: A DANGEROUS CHARACTER

1. Stevenson list, *New York Times,* January 25, 1919, 1:4.
2. Baker telegram, January, 1919, and Wald to Schwarz, Wald Papers, Reel 2, Box 3, NYPL.
3. Lusk Committee, Wald Papers, Box 97, COL.
4. Schiff to Wald's secretary, January 28, 1919, Wald Papers, COL.
5. 1919 trip to Europe, Wald Papers, Reel 2, Box 3, NYPL. At Zurich conference, "Report of the International Congress of Women," Zurich, May 12 to 17, 1919, Swarthmore College Peace Collection, Swarthmore, Pa.
6. Letters to the "family," Wald Papers, Reel 2, Box 3, NYPL.
7. Schiff telegram, June 15, 1920, Wald Papers, COL.
8. Walt Whitman, "Salut au Monde," Crowley, *The Neighborhood Playhouse,* pp. 121–132; Walt Whitman, *Leaves of Grass* (New York: A Modern Library Giant, Random House), p. 112, canto 7.
9. Postwar: Wald, *Windows on Henry Street,* p. 287; Hofstadter et al., *The American Republic,* Vol. 2, pp. 432–437; David Williams, "The Bureau of Investigation and its Critics, 1919–1921: The Origins of Federal Politi-

cal Surveillance," *The Journal of American History,* Vol. 68, No. 3, December 1981, pp. 560–567.

10. Wald to Dock, August 16, 1919; Wald to Waters, September 3, 1919, Wald Papers, Reel 2, Box 3, NYPL.

11. Schiff to Rockefeller, Adler, *Jacob Schiff,* p. 385; Wald to Rabinowitz, December 26, 1919; Wald Papers, Reel 2, NYPL.

12. Wald to Catt, September 4, 1919, Wald Papers, Reel 2, Box 3, NYPL.

13. Wald on Schiff's death, the *Survey,* October 2, 1920, p. 4; Schiff's gift, the *New York Sun,* July 6, 1921, 10:3.

14. Industrial Conference, 1919, Wald Papers, Reel 2, Box 3, NYPL; letter to the *Independent,* Reznick dissertation, p. 269.

15. Wald to Dock, 1920; Wald to New York Mission Society, January 6, 1923, Wald Papers, Reel 2, Box 3, NYPL.

16. Changes in settlements, see Donna Bonem, Susan Goldman, Hugh Strauss, "The Professional Consciousness of Social Work" (Master of Social Work thesis, Hunter College School of Social Work, 1975); Walter I. Trattner, *From Poor Law to Welfare State; A History of Social Welfare in America* (New York: Free Press, 1974), pp. 154–156; pp. 208–225; Davis, *Spearheads for Reform,* pp. 228–232.

17. Lovers of Freedom, New York *Call,* October 15, 1920, pp. 1, 2.

18. Surveillance of Miss Wald, information received from the United States Justice Department under the Freedom of Information Act; mentioned is Wald's support of the American Society for Cultural Relations with Russia of which she was vice-president, and the American Association for Labor Legislation of which she was vice-president. In material relating to President Franklin D. Roosevelt aide Harry Hopkins, was remark that, "in New York he joined the radical coterie which gravitated around Lillian Wald and Florence Kelley (Wischnewetsky). . . ."

19. Wald's postwar activities, Wald Papers, Box 17, COL; Sacco and Vanzetti, Wald Papers, Box 30, COL; Massachusetts Governor Michael Dukakis issued a proclamation on 50th anniversary of their execution, stating that Sacco and Vanzetti were not treated justly in the judicial process and that any remaining stigma should be removed from their names, *New York Times,* July 19, 1977, 14:6.

20. 1924 trip to Europe, Wald Papers, Reel 2, Box 3, NYPL.

21. Wald to Uncle Sam, December 5, 1923, Wald Papers, Reel 2, Box 3, NYPL.

22. Trip to Mexico, Wald Papers, Reel 2, Box 1–2, NYPL.

23. On surgery, Dock telegram to Wald, April 28, 1925; Kelley to Wald, May 1925; Dock to Wald, May 10, 1925, Wald Papers, Box 14, COL.

24. On purchase of Henry Street Playhouse, see Abrons, *My Life,* p. 128.

25. *The Dybbuk,* Wald Papers, Reel 2, Box 3, NYPL; Crowley, *The Neighborhood Playhouse,* pp. 199–218; on Tagore, p. 60.

26. Segal-Siegel interview, October 17, 1981; Sokolow-Siegel interview, November 7, 1981.

Chapter 14: "WHERE THE WINDS DO BLOW"

1. House-on-the-Pond, Wald Papers, misc. collection, COL.
2. The Economic Depression, Wald, *Windows on Henry Street,* pp. 231 ff; Duffus, *Lillian Wald,* pp. 291–294.
3. Her will, Wald Papers, Box 16, COL.
4. *New York World Telegram,* December 1930, Wald Papers, Box 1–2, NYPL; Wald to Harry Spector, November 9, 1929, Wald Papers, Box 42, COL.
5. Birthday greetings, Wald Papers, Box 16, COL; "Forty Years on Henry Street," the *Survey,* May 1933, No. 5, p. 192.
6. Dock letters to Nutting, File 1, Drawer 1, TC.
7. Retirement as Head Resident, Wald Papers, Reel 1, Box 1–2, NYPL.
8. Rubman-Siegel interview, July 8, 1981.
9. Wald to Abrons, February 19, 1935, H. L. Abrons Collection.
10. Wald to Mrs. Rockefeller quoted in Duffus, *Lillian Wald,* p. 312; to Bath, New York, p. 312; to Eleanor Roosevelt, p. 322.
11. Goldmark, *Impatient Crusader,* p. 208.
12. N.Y. City playground, *New York Times,* March 10, 1937, 17:1, 70th birthday celebration, Wald Papers, Reel 1, Box 1–2, NYPL; New York *Jewish Examiner,* March 6, 1937; *New York Times Magazine* feature article, March 7, 1937, VIII, p. 9.
13. Wald to Cohen family, March 12, 1937, Rubman Collection.
14. Wald to Lehman, February 16, 1939, Herbert H. Lehman Papers, Columbia University.

EPILOGUE

Randall to Dock, March 7, 1947, Dock Papers, LC.

Index